**Praise for *Why Study History?***

This book sets out the intellectual, economic and societal benefits of studying history at university. It offers a brilliant guide to choosing the right course, from the type of history on offer to selecting the institution best suited to you. I recommend it to all students and their parents as they plan their next steps.

*Holly Hiscox, history teacher,*
*d'Overbroeck's Sixth Form, Oxford*

This book is a really important read for history students in key stages 4 and 5. It clearly and accessibly dispels the notion that the only career options for a historian are as a teacher or a lecturer. I look forward to seeing both an upsurge in history degree applications from my students and a diversification of their career choices after reading this book!

*Annabelle Larsen, Head of Humanities,*
*Moat Community College, Leicester*

An excellent guide for students of history – why to study history, how to study it, where to study it, what it can do for you in your future worklife, for your personal development, and for the public good. This short guide busts a lot of myths and offers practical advice based on an unparalleled understanding of how history is actually taught on both sides of the Atlantic, in schools and universities.

*Peter Mandler, University of Cambridge*

This brief volume is packed with wisdom and practical advice. Students of history – young and old – will find much of value in its pages.

*Sam Wineburg, author of* Why Learn History
(When It's Already on Your Phone)

*Why Study History?* offers an invaluable guide to 'everything you wanted to know about studying history, but were perhaps afraid to ask'. This unusual and unusually useful handbook surefootedly leads the prospective student and aspiring historian through every conceivable step in the process from the first glint of interest in a student's eye, to the selection of a course of study, to life as a professional academic. Stearns and Collins methodically bust myths and offer sound advice based on decades of teaching and mentoring experience. Yet for all its sober and sensible practicality, the authors successfully convey the joy of history.

*Mary Lindemann, Professor and Chair,*
*Department of History, University of Miami*

At last, we have a volume that directly challenges the doubts and apprehensions many students have about studying history. Collins and Stearns bring to bear decades of experience addressing these questions in the classroom, and place that alongside the latest data to demonstrate the tangible value studying the past can bring over a lifetime. Much needed and highly recommended.

*Robert B. Townsend,*
*American Academy of Arts and Sciences*

If those who are unable to remember the past are doomed to repeat it, then students of history are best placed to learn from its mistakes. As this book sets out in lucid detail, the study of history is not only a fascinating personal endeavour but a profound public good, essential for policymaking, scientific inquiry and cultural progress. The skills I learned at university have accompanied me throughout my career, and I would recommend history to all.

*Will Tanner, BA History (2010), University College London,*
*founding director of the thinktank Onward and formerly*
*Deputy Head of Policy in 10 Downing Street*

# WHY STUDY HISTORY?

## The *Why Study* Series

Studying any subject at degree level is an investment in the future that involves significant cost. Now more than ever, students and their parents need to weigh up the potential benefits of university courses. That's where the *Why Study* series comes in. This series of books, aimed at students, parents and teachers, explains in practical terms the range and scope of an academic subject at university level and where it can lead in terms of careers or further study. Each book sets out to enthuse the reader about its subject and answer the crucial questions that a college prospectus does not.

**Published**

*Why Study History?* — Marcus Collins and Peter N. Stearns

**Forthcoming**

*Why Study Geography?* — Alan Parkinson
*Why Study Languages?* — Gabrielle Hogan-Brun
*Why Study Mathematics?* — Vicky Neale

# WHY STUDY HISTORY?

BY MARCUS COLLINS AND PETER N. STEARNS

Published by London Publishing Partnership
www.londonpublishingpartnership.co.uk

All Rights Reserved

ISBN: 978-1-913019-04-4 (pbk)

A catalogue record for this book is
available from the British Library

This book has been composed in Kepler Std

Copy-edited and typeset by
T&T Productions Ltd, London
www.tandtproductions.com

Printed and bound in Great Britain
by Hobbs the Printers Ltd

**Cover image**

*Launched by the Soviet Union in October 1957, Sputnik 1 – as
shown on the cover – was the first artificial Earth satellite.
It represents both a major milestone in the exploration of
space and a significant event in the Cold War, triggering
a new era of competition with the United States. It also
led to the development of dramatic new methods of global
communication based on satellite transmission: perhaps its
most important contribution to world history to date.*

# CONTENTS

CONTENTS

**PART IV**
**HISTORY AS A PUBLIC GOOD**

# ACKNOWLEDGEMENTS

Many thanks go to Richard Baggaley, Alan Booth, Sam Clark, Mersey Collins, Mike Goddard, Rachel Hewitt, Eoin MacGabhann, Luke Perrott, Paul Sturtevant, Ellen White and the anonymous reviewer.

# CHAPTER 1

Getting started: making the most of history

HISTORY IS, OR CAN BE, immensely practical, and it opens a wide variety of career doors. It also enlightens life.

*By all means study history. [It] is an endless source of fascination and very good company when the world seems to be going to hell around you.*[1]

That's what a chief executive in an American utility company had to say about why people should study history. He majored in history as an undergraduate and found it directly relevant to his successful career in management:

*Software changes even more rapidly than computer chips, but determining what is changing rapidly, what is changing slowly, and how people respond to the pace of change requires a particular skill-set – and these are the kinds of questions addressed squarely by historians.*

A successful lawyer, who also studied history at university, agrees:

*In a world of rapid economic change, the ability to grasp and explain the meaning of change is a skill of significant value in the marketplace.*

He notes history's value in 'creating openness to the ideas of others with different experiences, information and views' so that it 'provides support for social responsibility, engaged citizenship and the institutions of democratic societies'. When asked to answer the question addressed by this book – why study history? – he replied:

*A better question would be, why not study history?*[2]

## The basic argument

This book lays out the ways in which studying history provides intellectual value, enhances citizenship and prepares students for a range of careers. It discusses the principal fields of historical study at universities today, outlines what to look for in choosing particular history programmes and offers a guide on how to make the transition from school to college. The intent is to explore history's rich promise while providing a practical guide for students and their advisors. It's designed to help university applicants write their personal statements and prepare for their admissions interviews.

There are three main reasons to study history:

(1) Many students simply like it. They may like it because they were exposed to historical stories growing up, or because they had a beguiling history teacher in high school, or because they find trying to figure out what life was like in the past intriguing. It's not always clear why one likes a subject, but preferences should not be discounted. As this book will show, students who choose to follow their passions into university are likely to be rewarded by the exceptionally high standards of teaching provided by history faculties.

(2) It's a great way to think about the human condition and get an active sense of why the current climate is the way that it is. Comparing the present with the past and charting major processes of change and continuity builds a vital understanding of how people think and behave, and how previous patterns have evolved. These skills are becoming increasingly important in today's 'post-truth' society.

(3) It prepares students for a wide variety of careers, and recent surveys demonstrate that these careers yield competitive salaries and impressive levels of job satisfaction. The skills developed by studying history are in high demand, across an array of professions and occupations.

This book will pay a great deal of attention to reasons (2) and (3), which should sit at the core of any student's decision as to whether (and where) to study history at university.

## The jobs scene

To begin, let's deal with a few common misconceptions; more elaborate explanations will follow in later chapters. In recent years, especially since the Great Recession of 2008, many applicants to university have assumed that the only really safe career choice is a degree in one of the fabled STEM (science, technology, engineering, mathematics) fields, and that a subject like history doesn't cut it as a practical option. Now, there's nothing wrong with studying STEM subjects, but the assumptions about history simply aren't true. Average incomes for history graduates don't just compare well with those who studied degrees in the arts, humanities and social sciences. They match the incomes of graduates in some scientific fields and aren't far behind those of business graduates. Those who progress from a history degree into management or law, as many do, can earn substantial salaries.

So, why do misapprehensions abound in the jobs domain? One reason is that in difficult economic times it's easy to overestimate the value of 'practical' degrees and underestimate the value of degrees like history that lead to diverse career paths. While history prepares students for a range of professions, many of these do not follow as directly from their degree as is true in, say, engineering, and this complicates generalizations about jobs. Lots of history graduates carve out careers in fields where you wouldn't expect to find historians, but where the skills developed as part of a history degree are, in fact, highly valued.

Chapter 3 offers precise data on salaries and job satisfaction, and shows why choosing to focus on history is an entirely practical decision. Other parts of the book will explain how to evaluate a history programme, including its resources for career advice and placements. The next chapter explores the varied skills that studying history develops. This is a key reason why history graduates do so well in a disparate job market, and a vital point for history students to remember when they are explaining why they are job-ready. These students have reason to be proud of the various ways they contribute to society and the economy as well as the personal rewards that result from their work.

## The limits of school history

Besides the jobs issue, many of the chapters in this book confront another potential area of confusion: the relationship between history at school and at university level. It is vital to note the success of many school history courses – a success that has surely motivated many of the readers of this book. Many secondary teachers are immensely knowledgeable and enthusiastic, and they help produce students who are eager for more. It's also true, however, that school-based impressions of what studying history involves are often off the mark, in part because the field has changed quite rapidly in recent decades. School history, for various reasons, has often not kept up with history as an innovative discipline, to some extent because good teachers are not themselves fully in charge of their curriculum.

Two misapprehensions are particularly common among under-graduates. The first is that the study of history is mainly about memorization: that it's all names and dates. This has never been true, and it's even less true now that so many data are readily available through online sources. Good memories help in history, as in any field, and it's true that some hard-pressed history teachers spend more time testing their students on factual retention than they should (or than most of them really want to). Nevertheless, history is mainly about interpretation and analysis. How can one recognize a valid source of information, or allow for bias? How can the causes of change be determined, or at least be plausibly discussed? How can we identify and explain durable continuities from the past, such as Western individualism or the persistent inequality that has bedevilled most societies over the past 4,000 years? How, quite simply, can persuasive written or oral arguments be built from data? History students spend a lot of time writing – a measurable job asset – precisely because they are learning to argue from evidence and answer complex questions. The study of history is really about gaining habits of mind, not winning prizes for factual retention. History trains future leaders to succeed in business or politics or teaching rather than on quiz shows.

The second misapprehension is that history has a limited subject matter and is focused on kings and queens, presidents and prime ministers, wars and battles, with a few leading intellectuals tossed in. History does seek a better understanding of political change, and it has a lot to say about how wars can best be conducted or avoided. And it certainly pays a lot of attention to the importance of power structures. However, when we surveyed first-year undergraduates, they contrasted the multiplicity of themes, sources and interpretations studied at university with the top-down political history they'd learned in school. 'Throughout my time at school I have only been taught traditional history, under the impression that this is the only way to study history,' one commented. Another student confessed to 'feeling cheated' by the narrow focus of his school's history curriculum. 'There is more to life than that, and there is more to history than that,' he concluded.[3]

There is indeed. This is why historians have been at the forefront of a real explosion in subject matter in recent years. They are as interested in women as they are in men, in the LGBT+ community as they are in heterosexuals, and in the ruled and conquered as much as in rulers and conquerors. They offer histories of human impact on the environment as well as of the evolution of ideas about happiness and well-being. They use historical analysis to promote a better understanding of human emotions, or why sports garner such impassioned attention in modern societies. There is no subject of any importance that is off the table if it deals with people and human society. This means that history has become a source of major discoveries about conditions of human life and about how the past is shaping the present. In the process, good history programmes have also expanded to embrace many regions of the world, and not, as was still often true 50 years ago, primarily the West. For good measure, many historians have become adept at using digital media to analyse data and to present their findings to a contemporary public.

In fact, one of the reasons to study history is to catch up with the varied findings and debates that form the core of current research and teaching – and even, as student researchers, to participate in further innovation. The vast range of topics covered by history is one of the reasons it prepares students for so many different job options. It also steadily expands history's service in making life more interesting by adding to the perspectives on how human beings think and act.

## History and public needs

The study of history provides public benefits, addressing issues that are becoming increasingly important today. This is why a number of distinguished commentators, both conservative and liberal, are urging a rededication to history teaching and learning. Historical training helps people to handle different kinds of evidence and to sort fact from opinion and disinformation. It inevitably exposes students to different interpretations, promoting better methods of evaluating – and also reconciling – diverse points of view. In our era, when we are surrounded by fraudulent claims and intensely partisan disagreements, these skills are becoming particularly valuable. Research shows that people with historical training are far better than average at both detecting fake news and discounting it.[4]

Furthermore, as the quotes that opened this chapter suggested, historical study has a strong focus on the nature of change. We live in rapidly changing and challenging times. History immerses us in examples of change, from the ancient to the recent. History students learn to evaluate magnitudes of change, or the differences between real shifts in direction and adjustments along existing trend lines. They know that change is almost always complicated by important survivals from the past, which can help them sort out the swirl of changes around us today. Whether the change involved is some aspect of globalization, or some new objection to traditional democratic institutions, or the new standards the Me Too movement is urging in the area of sexual behaviour, historical training is central to figuring out what is going on.

## The book's structure

This book describes what the current study of history is about – what it covers, what purposes it serves, and how it connects both to successful careers and to a better society. It discusses the issues involved in evaluating university history programmes, getting into them and taking maximum advantage of what they offer. It's written by two historians who love the past, but who have no interest in producing a mindless advertisement for the discipline. Choosing to study history is an eminently sensible decision. It can be an exciting one, opening unexpected opportunities for learning and research as well as professional and personal growth, but it should be undertaken with a real appreciation of what the discipline is about: as a subject area, as part of responsible citizenship and as a source of job preparation. This book seeks to enhance that understanding.

The chapter following this introduction deals with basic modes of historical thinking and presentation, and some common confusions about what historical work is all about. In Chapter 3, we turn to careers for history graduates and the value of degree-level historical skills in the workplace. Chapters 4 and 5 survey categories of historical study: time periods, places and topical concentrations, and their connection to society today. Chapter 6 relates these categories to the teaching offered in history programmes so that students can make an informed choice about what to study and where to study it. Chapter 7 explores how undergraduates experience the study of history and how they can make the most of their work in the field. Chapter 8 considers the social contribution of historical analysis. We offer some final thoughts in our Conclusion.

The authors bring to this book different experiences, perspectives and areas of expertise. This means that, although the book is very much a collaborative enterprise, one of us (PS) is primarily responsible for Chapters 1, 3, 4, 5 and 8 and the other (MC) is primarily responsible for Chapters 2, 6 and 7. All chapters address the similarities and differences between the study of history in the US and Britain, where we respectively live and work. The internationalism of the historical profession is one of its great virtues, but it's nonetheless important to acknowledge the different structures and traditions of higher education in the UK and the US, which is reflected in correspondingly different terminology. George Bernard Shaw's observation almost a century ago that Britain and America are 'two countries separated by the same language' still applies today. For simplicity's sake, we'll use a single set of terms throughout the book:

| | |
|---|---|
| *Graduate* | *Alumnus or alumna of a Bachelor of Arts (BA) programme* |
| *Humanities* | *The study of human experience, action and creation (AKA arts and humanities)* |
| *Major* | *A chosen field of study* |
| *Module* | *An individual university course taken for credit* |
| *Postgraduate* | *Graduate student studying for master's (MA) or doctorate (PhD)* |
| *Programme* | *Program (AKA degree – or sometimes, and rather confusingly, course)* |
| *Secondary school* | *High school and junior high* |
| *University* | *College* |

Differences between UK and US experiences and terminology need to be recognized, but this book also emphasizes how the study of history, and the value of studying it, are similar on both sides of the Atlantic. While historians from many nations have contributed to the current dynamism of historical research and teaching, American and British innovations and discoveries have played a vital role. This book, addressing a transatlantic audience, builds on these connections.

Now we've explained what we're saying and how we're saying it, it's time to consider the case for studying history in more depth. One of the great joys of being a historian at university level is the opportunity it presents to work with undergraduates, and this book seeks to return the favour. History contributes to a greater understanding of human life, whatever career one chooses, and ultimately this is the main point.

*Further reading*

There is a rich literature on the reasons to study history. The revised edition of R. G. Collingwood's *The Idea of History* (Oxford: Oxford University Press, 1994) and Marc Bloch's *The Historian's Craft: Reflections on the Nature and Uses of History and the Techniques and Methods of Those Who Write It* (New York: Alfred A. Knopf, 1953) are two classic statements, both by eminent practitioners. For a recent take, and for comments on how history is and should be taught, see Sam Wineburg's *Why Learn History (When It's Already on Your Phone)* (Chicago, IL: University of Chicago Press, 2018). To get some ideas about job prospects, visit the 'Careers for historians' page on the American Historical Association's website (https://bit. ly/3c2yc8h).

# PART I

SKILLS AND JOBS:
THE RESULTS OF HISTORICAL STUDY

# CHAPTER 2

Meeting needs: the reasons to study history

HISTORY IS THE STUDY OF the past, but its goal is to improve our understanding of the present – and sometimes even to offer glimpses into the future. History's utility rests on two basic facts. First, history is the fullest laboratory we have for data and examples of how people and societies function. Second, historical study generates a number of skills that are directly relevant to all sorts of professional activities, capped by a unique perspective on understanding the process of change.

This chapter considers why historical knowledge and methods of analysis are vital assets for individuals and societies alike. To maintain that history is valuable is not to diminish the *pleasure* of historical study. Many of us read history books or watch historical documentaries simply for the joy of knowing more about the human condition. Exploring how men and women lived in the past – how different from us they are, but also how unexpectedly similar, despite specific circumstance – is enriching and fascinating.

Yet the study of history does more than satisfy our curiosity. Without a profound understanding of the past, societies, organizations and individuals will make needless mistakes and fail to take full advantage of emerging opportunities. We all use historical experience in our daily lives. We remember things we did wrong in the past and should probably not repeat, or we repeat past mistakes because we don't take our own histories seriously. Alternatively, we remember things that worked well and might therefore shape our choices for the better in future. Studying the history of groups, organizations or whole societies takes our opportunities to benefit from the past to another level. It's almost impossible for people *not* to look to history, and this means there's every reason to learn how to study it well.

## The human laboratory

There are real constraints on how much we can experiment with human societies. There are, of course, a few limited opportunities for experiments with new social programmes in order to see if they work locally before applying them more widely, and psychologists run a variety of laboratories to see how individuals behave in certain circumstances. However, on most of the big issues societies or organizations face, we can't responsibly fiddle around. We can't start a war merely to gain information about how mass casualties affect a society or what tactics work best, for example. We can sometimes look to the experience of other societies – comparative social science is a vital companion to history – but the availability of history to provide data and examples of human behaviour is absolutely crucial.

As a result, people who know how to get at these data and make sense of the information – historians, in other words – are indispensable. Use of historical information and examples to help shape current decisions takes a variety of specific forms, which are explored in the sections that follow. Our basic point is that history gives us information about how to promote peace, or maintain democracy, or see how families react to urban life. In all sorts of arenas, it's far better to know history than to strike out blindly.

This history-as-human-laboratory point is no mere abstraction. Contemporary crises remind us that we need information from the past to help us deal with current uncertainties. Among the first questions raised by the Covid-19 (coronavirus) disruption in 2020 were: What features of previous epidemics can provide societies today with greater understanding and guidance? What's new about the current challenge? What's fairly typical? We'll come back to this example in Chapter 8.

## Moral understanding

This is one of the oldest categories for drawing lessons from historical data. The fact is that studying the stories of individuals and situations in the past allows a history student to test his or her own moral sense, to hone it on some of the real complexities that individuals have faced in challenging settings. People who have weathered adversity not just in some work of fiction but in real historical circumstances can provide insight and even inspiration. So, too, can stories of success, which is why business students examine historical case studies of dynamic or socially responsible firms.

'History is philosophy teaching by example' is one phrase that describes this use of studying the past.[5] At its most conventional, history involves the study of famous men and women who successfully worked through hardships and moral dilemmas. But history students also explore the lives of ordinary people, who provide lessons in courage, diligence or successful protest. History is one of very few courses that really encourages students to put themselves in other people's shoes, to develop what is sometimes called a 'sympathetic imagination' beyond the boundaries of personal values and experiences. It can be argued that, particularly in our increasingly diverse and globalized world, this capacity is a vital moral asset.

## Avoiding mistakes

One of the most frequently quoted aphorisms applied to history is a 1905 statement by the philosopher George Santayana:

*Those who cannot remember the past are condemned to repeat it.*[6]

A recent poll of some older Americans taking history courses in retirement learning centres revealed a version of the same sentiment. They particularly liked history because it provided examples of really bad periods in the past – a reminder that however dark things seem today, they could be worse – as well as cases in which mistakes were made that we can and should avoid today.[7] Thus, military strategists frequently study past battles, and teach budding officers about them, precisely because of wrong decisions that shouldn't be repeated.[8] Chinese leaders have carefully studied the history of the fall of the Soviet Union, determined not to repeat what they see as policy mistakes in the 1980s, and arguably they have learned quite a bit. The history of business organizations provides similar lessons: why was the Kodak photography company so slow to realize the implications of technological change, and what can we draw from this to guide more successful behaviour?

This category – learning about mistakes we should avoid, in all sorts of areas – is admittedly easier to preach about than to translate into practice. History is replete with examples of decisions that could've easily been avoided if the past had been heeded. For example, the American invasion of Iraq in 2003 arguably repeated the blatantly misguided assumptions already proven wrong in Vietnam. The current rise of anti-Semitism, in both Europe and the US, raises questions about whether people today adequately remember the moral horrors of the Nazi regime. But there are more salutary examples as well. Most Americans have learned from history that the mistreatment of Japanese Americans in World War II was wrong, and this affects their response to more recent crises such as the 9/11 terrorist attack – although the subject of internment still provokes controversy. As Santayana said, it really is inexcusable not to use the past to help us avoid mistakes. It takes historians to explore the relevant examples and suggest the lessons we must learn.

## Using analogies

In historical study, analogies are attractive because they compare something unknown – like a very recent event – to a well-studied case from the past that seems to be similar enough to provide an informative model.[9]

Thus, when something unexpected or troubling happens in an organization or society, it's almost essential to ask if there's any past instance that provides a useful perspective. For example, a couple of decades ago, when computers were just making inroads in the classroom, a university president compared the potential impact of these devices to that of steam engines on manufacturing two centuries earlier. More recently, when newly elected President Donald Trump made it clear that he would govern rather differently from his predecessors, many people asked historians if there were cases of this kind of behaviour earlier in the American experience. The implicit hope was that if we could calibrate the present by a known example from the past, it might provide some guidance on how to handle current challenges more successfully. Another example is even more specific: in 2017, when nuclear tensions between the US and North Korea were mounting, a historian called attention to the Cuban missile crisis of 1962, urging leaders to see that event as an example of how to de-escalate a dangerous confrontation. The crisis and its peaceful resolution featured some attitudes and behaviours that could be imitated.[10]

More broadly, one of the clear functions of history is to help us avoid wild or misleading claims about the novelty of the world around us. Few historians would agree with the aphorism that there's nothing new under the sun, as this contradicts our grasp of change. However, they certainly love to puncture excessive or anxious characterizations of new trends by comparing them to similar examples from the past. The result may provide only a very general sense of perspective, but it's better than thinking there's no relevant precedent to help guide us amid innovation.

Using historical cases for perspective has a flip side, however, which is equally important. Because people so often look for past examples to guide us in unfamiliar circumstances, it's easy to go overboard with claims of resemblance. Often, knowledgeable historians are essential in cutting through the confusion. For at least a generation, Western diplomats thought they 'knew' from the events leading up to World War II that initiatives by authoritarian regimes should always be opposed using force. After all, in 1938 British leaders had thought they could conciliate Hitler at a famous conference in Munich by sanctioning the annexation of part of Czechoslovakia on the understanding that he would not ask for more. Within months, he had swallowed the whole nation, and all the West could do was impotently watch.

There's widespread agreement that a policy of appeasement was doomed to failure, but post-war policymakers' determination to avoid 'another Munich' created problems of its own. The US took military action against the communist uprising in Vietnam in part because of what American leaders remembered about Britain's failure to stand up against Hitler's aggression. However, by this point, a new breed of diplomatic historians were beginning to realize that the Munich analogy was potentially misleading, and that current patterns might only be superficially similar to those on the eve of World War II.[11] History helps to orient us by considering past developments that may shed light on otherwise mystifying present-day changes. But it can also warn us against oversimplification. Either way, an informed understanding of historical precedent provides a vital service to the modern world.

## History and identity

Group identity and history are inevitably intertwined. This is one reason that all modern nations encourage history being taught in schools: to provide a reasonably coherent narrative of the nation's development, its key events and institutions and its (real or imagined) distinguishing characteristics. A sense of national identity provides a vital element of citizenship.

At the other extreme, many people delight in studying the history of their own families (encouraged more recently by genetic testing). This promotes family cohesion and an appreciation of how their family has interacted with larger historical patterns such as migrations or wars. Many institutions – businesses, localities, etc. – use history for similar purposes of establishing identity. Historical work has been vital in shaping a sense of working-class experience and identity in Britain, along with ethnic identity there and in the US. The rise of second-wave feminism in the 1960s was intertwined with a wholesale historical reassessment of women's experiences, creating an intimate link between contemporary gender identities and historical research. LGBT+ identity has been similarly forged by reclaiming the past in order to comprehend the present and chart a better future.

Our point is that any purely presentist definition of a group has little meaning. Group identity gains substance when it's grounded upon a shared understanding of the past, including prior successes and challenges. However, while identity needs and issues form legitimate subjects for historical inquiry, they also harbour some challenges to accuracy and objectivity. The politicization of identity can distort the complexity of the past. National histories, usually bent on glorifying the nation and emphasizing distinctive strengths, can become propagandistic. All groups, including nations, are to some degree socially and culturally invented, which should invite some caution from historians lest any contemporary form of identity be seen as simply inevitable. However, such challenges in no way detract from history's basic importance in fleshing out and explaining identity claims.[12]

## Origins of the present

Another way in which history provides data and analysis vital to public understanding is that it can explain the origins and evolution of current phenomena that may otherwise seem 'natural' or, at the other extreme, purely contemporary, and therefore not in need of any particular inquiry. Exploring the emergence of national political practices is one example, but this branch of historical research is so much broader than that.

Take, for instance, the problem of loneliness. A great deal of attention is currently devoted to loneliness – Britain's Department for Digital, Culture, Media and Sport added a strategy for tackling loneliness to its agenda in 2018 – and there is sound research on the role ageing and social media play in exacerbating the problem. A striking new study, still being elaborated, adds an unexpected historical component to this seemingly contemporary issue: it claims that the modern meaning of loneliness actually began to emerge in the later eighteenth century. Of course, recent technological developments have added more complexity to the historical picture, but it's clear from this study that they should be juxtaposed with the larger chronology. Loneliness is neither entirely natural nor entirely novel, and this is where a historical perspective becomes essential.[13]

A very different example is nationalism, which is a divisive contemporary phenomenon that can't be understood if detached from its historical roots. Recognizably modern nationalism also began in the eighteenth century – which is when the first explicitly national anthem saw the light of day – but it has gone through a number of permutations since then. For instance, by the later nineteenth century it had shifted from a primarily liberal to an often-conservative ideology. Being able to capture the passions and tensions of contemporary nationalism, then, depends on our grasp of its historical trajectory.

Tracing and explaining the present through the past obviously gives precedence to fairly recent developments, but earlier patterns may come into play. Many historians argue that a distinctive attitude towards nature began to emerge in the Mediterranean world around the time of the ancient Greeks and the development of Judaism. In contrast to Indian and African or Native American traditions, this belief system stressed a separation between humankind and the rest of nature in ways that help to explain our distinctive willingness to exploit the environment. This is a big claim that warrants further discussion, but it suggests that one aspect of the current environmental crisis may require us to interrogate a historical perspective that goes back over two millennia.[14]

Many observers point to the strong emphasis on happiness that's seemingly characteristic of modern Western cultures. A recent poll showed a marked contrast between Western parents, who listed their children's happiness as their chief goal, and parents elsewhere, who placed greater emphasis on achievement or health.[15] This aspect of Western culture goes back to the eighteenth century, too, when cheerfulness began to be emphasized as a vital requirement. It gained further traction in the middle of the nineteenth century, which is when the modern concept of birthday parties first took hold, followed by the emergence of the classic 'Happy Birthday' song in the early decades of the twentieth century. Thus, understanding contemporary happiness – and the problems associated with our excessive expectations surrounding it – requires us to look back at a history that began 250 years ago.[16]

A similar timescale applies to improving our understanding of other societies. No approach to contemporary China, for example, would be complete without paying attention to the Communist revolution that won out in 1949, or to the tremendous global reorientation and demographic shifts that began in 1978. But almost any expert on China will also highlight the need to grasp some elements of Confucian culture, which took shape over two millennia ago and which still, although much modified, helps to explain distinctive features of the culture today.

Figuring out how the present emerged from the past, then, does not rely on an examination of modern history alone. Our main point remains: much of the present is caused by the past, which is a crucial reason for knowing the connections involved. Using history to understand ourselves and the society around us – aside from the pleasure of thinking about the past for its own sake – clearly has a number of dimensions, from setting a moral example to helping us analyse the origins of contemporary trends or issues. Listing the connections may seem easy, but most require extensive research and discussion. This is precisely why historians and history students are essential, and why the study of history at university level opens so many doors to understanding.

Societies can't function without history. We can't explain ourselves, or our identities, or our mistakes without recourse to the past. The Roman philosopher Cicero argued:

*To be ignorant of what occurred before you were born is to remain always a child.*

This is a statement that applies to individuals and societies alike.[17]

Here, then, is half an answer to the questions of what history is all about and how it prepares people for the workforce. Before turning to the other half of the answer – the nature of historical thinking and its related skills – there's a further issue that's paramount in this day and age: our need for connection to the past leaves us open to manipulation.

## Fake news

Historical training is essential in producing people, in various careers, who can cut through misrepresentations of the past. Using history to serve our present needs depends on a commitment to the greatest possible accuracy and objectivity. Precisely because history is essential for contemporary explanation and identity, it can be distorted easily, whether casually or intentionally.

Thus, nations – most obviously in modern times – routinely reinvent aspects of history to suit their purposes. Hence the claim repeated in American classrooms well into the twentieth century that the US had never started but also never lost a war, which was blatantly untrue even aside from the country's recent misadventures. More commonly, the national guardians of history in schools simply pick and choose which bits to focus on, emphasizing the most favourable aspects of the national experience and downplaying or sugar-coating the rest. Organizational histories can be as selectively inaccurate as nationalist textbooks. Histories of the working class, for instance, long downplayed characteristic sexism, seeking only the most positive picture possible. That's not to mention such notorious lies as pretending the Holocaust never happened, or that Americans slaves laboured happily on the plantations.

This, then, offers another reason that historical study remains essential. Obviously, a wide popular interest in history is truly desirable, but there's an ongoing need for trained practitioners who cite accuracy as their key goal, who know how to collect relevant data and interpret it fairly, and who are willing to modify their assumptions in light of the available evidence.

That same impulse which labels current reporting as 'fake news' because it doesn't fit a particular agenda easily applies to the past. Authoritarianism thrives on distorting the past and its relationship to the present in order to create loyalty to a current regime and vilify opposing views.[18] It's always tempting to cherry-pick history: to use the past to service a particular power structure or cultural preference. Even in relatively open contemporary societies, increasingly vicious partisanships create opportunities to concoct histories to support particular preferences. The notorious lawlessness of social media, where invented stories can spread like wildfire, brings its own challenges.

Debate and disagreement play an essential role in historical work; it's hard to claim certainty about many big issues from the past. However, a commitment to seeking accuracy, and a willingness to modify assumptions in light of new discoveries, is fundamental to the historical project. A serious study of history is vital to the health of contemporary societies. It may sound a bit pompous to insist that good history helps us seek the truth, but this is, in fact, the case.

Some historians, reacting to the fake news epidemic and the rise of authoritarianism, have experimented with more explicit training to deal with hoaxes. One, for example, introduced a course titled 'Lying about the past', which allowed students to deal with the components of fake histories and how these can be disseminated, while developing new capacities in evaluation.[19] History training may become increasingly relevant in promoting constructive scepticism and explicit attention to truth-seeking. This is another reason we need practitioners in a variety of careers who are equipped to apply historical knowledge and skills.

## Thinking like a historian: not a bad idea

A vital second facet of history learning, though intertwined with data about the past, highlights skills and habits of mind. Historical thinking, broadly construed, is fundamental to good historical work, and it's an essential part of truth-seeking. It also has wider applicability: long after students have forgotten some of the facts so painstakingly memorized in history classes, they'll retain the mental capacities that history promotes.

Historical skills, in turn, fall into two categories, both of which are productive: those habits of mind shared with several other disciplines, and those central to historical thinking specifically. This basic skills list is not new, but it's being articulated more explicitly as part of history's contemporary message and explored more systematically in the classroom. It's also a list that history students should be actively aware of, so they can both explain why they're studying history and emphasize the skills they're gaining to a wider audience – employers included.

*Finding data*

Any good history programme, after an introductory course or two, sets students to work seeking information in order to answer key questions about what happened in the past. Sometimes the focus is on uncovering material available in existing books and articles that needs to be pulled out and reassembled. This kind of evidence comes from what historians call secondary sources: works produced subsequent to the events they describe that offer their own interpretation of the evidence.

History programmes also offer opportunities to look for facts in primary sources: materials that were produced either contemporaneously with the events under consideration or subsequently by contemporaries of those events. Diaries, letters, parliamentary debate transcripts, courtroom records, treaties and diplomatic exchanges, quantitative data like census materials: the list of what constitutes a primary source defies easy summary. The point is that history students, through research seminars and independent projects, gain skills in finding materials, assessing their motivations and assumptions, and figuring out what other data are desirable in fleshing out an account. Experience interpreting the statements of past political leaders – sorting out the objective from the subjective – can be readily applied to contemporary data as well. Combining different kinds of evidence, including visual materials, helps to create a more detailed picture, too. These skills are central to the historian's craft, but they transfer easily to other kinds of inquiry. The ability to research is one of the main qualities that history graduates bring to a host of professional tasks. A proficiency in assessing data has become even more significant amid the flood of material and its manipulation that is the age of the internet.

*Mounting arguments*

Once the data have been assembled, the historian has to figure out how to present a coherent argument that not only combines and accurately conveys the facts, but also forms a meaningful statement. Moving from a simple summary of facts to a persuasive analysis that addresses some larger question is not as easy as it sounds. History students are given diverse opportunities to develop this talent.

*Assessing conflicting interpretations*

Historical study involves debate, and virtually any significant topic generates differing claims and viewpoints. Learning how to identify and evaluate clashing interpretations is an essential skill – relevant to careers and citizenship alike – for which history provides explicit training. The same applies to the testing of various, sometimes clashing, theories dealing with patterns of historical change or the role of culture in shaping human behaviour. The world around us is full of debate, and experience in evaluating conflicting views about the past and emerging with a coherent statement of one's own is a highly marketable skill.

*Writing and speaking*

Students write a lot in their history classes; this is the most obvious way to demonstrate skills in research and interpretation. Interestingly, employers typically rate writing among the top skills they seek, but don't always find, in prospective hires. History offers those who desire a creative outlet in writing the chance to use their talents, and those who aren't naturally inclined to write the opportunity to build up their expertise.

History courses also provide opportunities to develop one's public speaking skills, which are vital in all sorts of professional settings. Learning how to time a presentation, how to convey convincing arguments and how to use PowerPoint effectively (there are some real challenges here!) are all part of good history courses. Furthermore, in a growing number of them, oral presentations are part of team assignments, providing students with yet another transferable skill.

*Critical thinking*

Gaining experience in evaluating evidence and sorting through diverse interpretations builds critical thinking skills. History students need not become inveterate sceptics, but they certainly learn not to take claims at face value. They have ample opportunity to figure out what kinds of self-interest are behind many public statements. Seeing what's below the surface of incidents is one of the most rewarding elements of historical research and argument. Assessing historical analogies or exaggerated presentism is a superb way to combine the use of historical data with a capacity to evaluate arguments. This is another explicit application of critical thinking.

*The challenge of ambiguity*

Recent discussions have highlighted another feature of studying history that many employers have come to value: a certain degree of comfort with ambiguous situations. Many of the most interesting historical issues require juggling lots of different angles and accepting that drawing a definitive conclusion is not a straightforward process. Students who are exposed to this aspect of the human experience in the classroom, and in their own projects, have a real leg-up in dealing with what is glibly called 'the real world' later on.

The various skills that support successful work in the history classroom cultivate abilities that will serve people well in later professional life and, more broadly, in their lives as informed citizens. These skills aren't accidental: they're deliberately encouraged and evaluated as part of any good history programme. They go well beyond memorizing a batch of facts, for they're essential tools in understanding the past and conveying that understanding to others.

## Historical thinking

Work in history develops one final set of capacities that's distinctive to the discipline: the ability to identify and interpret change. When people talk about 'thinking like a historian', they sometimes refer to the ability to find and evaluate documents and other primary materials. But even more commonly, and even more desirably, they mean the ability to evaluate change. No other discipline, however significant in other respects, focuses so centrally on change; yet change, in all its complexity, surrounds us. This means that history offers students a distinctive edge in dealing with a crucial element of our social environment.

A good history programme gives students experience handling many types of change: changes in warfare, gender relations, the environment, political structures and the functions of government, popular culture, art and even child-rearing. The list is long. It presents students with the challenge of assessing change in different parts of the world and in different time periods. Some historians would go so far as to contend that history courses themselves should be evaluated not for the facts they convey but for the types of change to which they expose students.

There is, of course, no single formula for dealing with change; many history courses simply introduce students to different examples of change and let their experience accumulate. But it's possible to survey some historical approaches to change, beginning with the identification of turning points. Historians routinely talk about new time periods in their subject area – for example, how the Renaissance differed from the preceding European Middle Ages by introducing new artistic styles and political trends. What they mean by this is that a considerable change was in the works. Other changes are significant but less systematic or are exaggerated for rhetorical effect, as when advertisers and politicians claim that a new deodorant or the latest wave of immigration will revolutionize our lives. History students gain skill in assessing magnitudes of change, sorting out the smaller vicissitudes from basic shifts of direction in some aspect of human society.

Identifying the nature and scope of change leads us directly to the next step in the process: making the clearest possible statement about what the situation was *before* a change occurred. Too often, change is not clearly grounded in an accurate baseline. Learning how to develop a baseline is another area where historical study provides vital experience. If someone is claiming that a change was big but fails to show how it contrasts with previous patterns, their claim should be treated as suspect.

Historians also grapple with causation, that is, the factors which promoted a change in the first place. Pinpointing causes in human affairs is hard, for we can't tidily replicate behaviours in a laboratory to figure out exactly which factors prompt what adjustments; we can't start a revolution, for example, just to see what's involved. In fact, scientists often find it hard to replicate results even in highly controlled laboratory experiments. However, it's important to develop models of historical causation – and to gain experience in dealing with the inevitable debates that emerge – as part of figuring out what change is all about. Again, this capacity can be directly extended to contemporary life, as when we're trying to figure out what factors prompted the Brexit vote, or the emergence of

Trump-like populism in the US, or the current decline in birth rate of many societies around the world (all of which involve essentially historical questions). We're inquiring into causes all the time, and we should be doing that, but it's history that gives us a grounding in how to go about these inquiries.

Dealing with causes comes with a host of charms and challenges. It begins with selecting relevant data for analysis, as do all phases of evaluating change. With causation, however, there's also the need to separate from mere correlation: developments that occur at the same point in time but aren't directly linked. One classic example of correlation is the fact that murder rates go up when sales of ice cream increase. There's obviously no causal link here (Ben & Jerry do not pose a homicide threat); it's simply that both respond independently to warmer weather.

Context and preconditions must also be noted. For instance, the Industrial Revolution couldn't have occurred without an enormous supply of coal. However, a large coal supply alone couldn't have caused industrialization, for coal reserves had existed for millions of years. It was a necessary condition, then, but not an active ingredient.

Finally, most major developments respond to several factors, that is, to multiple causations. Temperature increase, for example, is not the only reason murder rates go up, otherwise the rates wouldn't change much decade upon decade. Correlation, context and multiplicity all represent elements we must build into causation discussions, both historically and in the present. The task is manageable, but it improves with experience while promoting overall analytical abilities.

Change also involves a consideration of continuity. While this is not as challenging as dealing with causation, it deserves attention – particularly in our modern culture, where we assume rapid flux. Change is almost never absolute, overwhelming every aspect of the past; in fact, historians shudder when they hear someone argue that 'everything changed' as the result of some event or new technology. Dealing with persistence, even amid change, is one of the trickiest aspects of historical thinking, because focusing on change usually seems more exciting than considering what elements endure. Yet the assignment is inescapable. Even outright revolutions, such as the French Revolution of 1789 or the Russian Revolution of 1917, leave many aspects of society intact. In the case of Russia, for example, the Bolsheviks soon came to rely on a secret police that was little different from the one they'd just overthrown, which had been viewed as one of the most retrograde elements of the tsarist regime. A really good question to ask in any change analysis is this: what seems to be persisting from before?

Historians deal not only with the nature of change and its causes, but also with its wider impacts as well. Take, for example, one of the key changes in modern life, which is now becoming global: the 'revolution' in child mortality, from societies where 30–50% of all children died before the age of 5 to the current situation where these rates are as low as 1–2%. This momentous change occurred between 1880 and 1920 in Western societies and deserves analysis in terms of both its causes and its lingering continuities. It also invites further assessment of the results: how has the experience of being a parent or a sibling changed now that other children in the family are less likely to die? How have reactions to a child's death, when it does occur, shifted now that the experience is so unusual? Trying to figure out the human results of big changes is one of the great joys of historical work, and it can carry over into assessments of change in the present as well.

Ambitious historians and history students also try to figure out when an initially novel trend stops, or when other priorities begin to overshadow its significance. To take a familiar case, the Renaissance, once a major change, eventually gave way to other cultural and political patterns. At some point during the twentieth century, the use of horses in warfare, once a huge historical innovation, yielded to other technologies. Newspapers, a huge new factor in the eighteenth and nineteenth centuries, in due course gave way to audio-visual media – a process that's still underway. Figuring out when an innovation trails off or when it's supplanted is a vital element of historical study.

Here, too, historical thinking invites application to the world around us. Almost by definition, we can't be sure what current trends are about to change their shape. But we can ask questions about the relationship of the present and probable near future to the recent past. For instance, Western culture in the nineteenth and twentieth centuries was unusually preoccupied with the qualities of youth, generating brand new concepts such as adolescence. Are we about to see this emphasis modified, as the percentage of elderly in the population soars? To take another case, the first two decades of the twenty-first century have seen a number of extremist attacks: at what point will fear of terrorism and the impact of 9/11 give way to other concerns? Again, we can't know for sure. But we *can* extend this aspect of historical thinking, at least, to ask good questions about the changes to come, and to monitor the results.

Here, then, is a clear and repeatable agenda for analysing change:

**Magnitude, baseline, causes, continuities, impacts and (possibly) endpoints or new transitions.**

It's an agenda that, whether explicitly or not, history students encounter when they deal with some of the larger issues in their history classes and research projects. Add historical thinking – the ability to evaluate change – to the other skills of research, argument building, critical thinking and presentation, and one emerges with a powerful package. It's a package that, combined with the sheer pleasure of considering the past, carries over into multiple career opportunities, which we'll cover in the next chapter. It's also a package that (many career forecasters contend) will prove unusually durable in the decades ahead, even amid the oscillations prompted by new technologies.[20]

## Utility and its discontents

Some historians may take issue with the arguments featured in this chapter, uncomfortable with having so much emphasis placed on history's practical side. There's an older tradition of history teaching which simply asserts that an 'educated person' must have some defined categories of factual knowledge, usually presented in terms of a Western canon, and that this is sufficient justification for historical study. This approach can also disapprove of there being too much emphasis on recent history, as opposed to the classics, or on the analysis of change; its advocates fear that what's often called the 'pastness of the past' may be sullied by too much connection with the needs of the present.

These concerns show up regularly in periodic laments that today's students don't know the essentials of American, British or Western history. Good history programmes can and do include opportunities to consider these objections, and – as we'll see in Chapter 4 – they may actively involve requirements designed to discourage too much presentism. Certainly, the opportunity to study past societies very different from our own – those that are more religious, for example

– can be truly instructive. There's no question that it's vital to have some historians who are committed to figuring out what medieval life was like, or uncovering the nature of the Islamic Golden Age, both to provide deeper perspectives on the present and to attract students fascinated by diverse pasts.

University programmes in any field are enriched by differences in priorities, as this help students figure out what disciplinary goals are most relevant for them and their own plans. That said, it remains legitimate to focus most of our attention on historical patterns and modes of analysis that help us explore the dynamics of the present as well as the past. Even historians who are devoted to earlier time periods actively encourage broader connections – for instance, when dealing with newer topics such as women's history – in order to offer precedents for this vital contemporary issue. They actively join with 'modernists' in working on the basic components of historical thinking, from assessment of evidence to attention to change. History's present-day utility, it seems, is inescapable.

A recent article makes this utility argument directly, highlighting the reasons humanities students do very well in medical careers and emphasizing the relevance of their critical thinking skills, their empathy and their tolerance of ambiguity alongside the scientific basics the medical field requires.[21] This is not a common connection, but it points once again to the wide applicability of historical knowledge and skills in dealing with contemporary social needs.

We hope it's now clear that the world today simply can't operate without historians and historical training, and it certainly shouldn't try to do so. Furthermore, historical training involves not only factual knowledge but also crucial habits of mind. History matters, and so do its students. We hope it's also clear that many career opportunities await those equipped with the skills acquired in a history course. Just what those opportunities are and how to make the most of them will be covered in our next chapter.

*Further reading*

A number of studies have explored the nature of historical thinking, often in relation to both student learning and employer demand; see Sam Wineburg's *Historical Thinking and Other Unnatural Acts* (Philadelphia, PA: Temple University Press, 2001) and Peter N. Stearns's *Meaning Over Memory* (Chapel Hill, NC: University of North Carolina Press, 1993). *Knowing, Teaching and Learning History*, edited by Peter N. Stearns, Peter Seixas and Sam Wineburg (New York: New York University Press, 2000), features essays from a variety of British and North American scholars. On discussions of historical thinking and how it might be evaluated, see Peter Seixas's and Tom Morton's *The Big Six Historical Thinking Concepts* (Boston, MA: Cengage Learning, 2012), which is derived from an important Canadian project.

# CHAPTER 3

Careers for history graduates

THIS CHAPTER PROVIDES CAREER INFORMATION useful to any student considering a degree or major in history. Here's the bottom line, and it's an encouraging one: history graduates are likely to have good careers and strong lifetime earnings. This is the message received from a number of recent surveys of graduates in history and related humanities subjects. Building on the skills they've gained by studying a rigorous and well-respected subject, history graduates land jobs in an impressive variety of fields and hold their own in terms of salary and career well-being.

Virtually nobody simply walks into their dream job these days. This chapter therefore outlines ways for history students to turn their time at university into a launch pad for their chosen career.

## The real data: career prospects, salaries and job satisfaction

The question of whether studying history will lead to a high-paying job is likely to preoccupy any student choosing a degree or major, not to mention their concerned parents. Over the past decade, many students appear to have calculated that a history degree is a risky investment. One important trigger for this way of thinking was the 2008 banking crisis and the years of economic austerity and instability that followed. Another probable cause has been the increasing cost of undergraduate degrees. Tuition fees tripled for English students entering university in 2012 and have recorded inflation-busting increases in most US institutions. Fearing for their prospects, and conscious of loan repayments, many undergraduates have gravitated towards degrees that seem to have more obvious career paths, such as business, medicine and law (or pre-med and pre-law).

But is this pessimism warranted? If you obtain a history degree, are you consigning yourself to a hardscrabble existence, just getting by, when another degree choice could have taken you places? Three enterprising historians – Ben Schmidt, Paul Sturtevant and Rob

Townsend – have sought to answer this question by taking a closer look at how history graduates fare in the US job market. Together, they make a powerful case for studying history, revealing that concerns about the employment prospects for graduates in history and the humanities are unfounded or exaggerated.

**Table 1** Careers of history alumni in the US, 2010–14. Figures courtesy of Paul B. Sturtevant and derived from an American Community Survey of individuals in the US aged 25-64 who were in full-time employment and who held a BA in history.

| | |
|---|---|
| Education, training and library science | 18.4% |
| Management: business, science and the arts | 15.2% |
| Legal occupations | 10.9% |
| Sales | 9.9% |
| Office and administrative support | 9.5% |
| Business operations | 4.6% |
| Arts, design, entertainment, sports and media | 4.1% |
| Community and social services | 3.7% |
| Financial services | 3.2% |
| Health care practitioners | 3.1% |
| ICT and mathematics | 2.8% |

Sturtevant looks to scotch the myths that history graduates are underemployed, underpaid and unprepared for the world of work, examining data collected by the US Census Bureau from 2010 to 2014 on the jobs historians do and the salaries they earn. He begins by investigating unemployment statistics. The proportion of history graduates aged between 25 and 64 who were out of work when surveyed was 4.6%, compared with 4.1% for degree-holders in general.[22] The difference of 0.5% isn't negligible, but look at it this way: this means (all things being equal) there's a 1 in 200 chance that choosing a history degree instead of an unspecified average degree will lead to a spell of joblessness. That's a really small risk compared with most of life's intangibles, particularly since there are many offsetting advantages to studying history.

Sturtevant also counters the notion that history majors are unprepared for work by showing the enormous range of careers in which they find themselves (see Table 1). If history students were trained for nothing but writing essays about Mughal emperors, he reasons, why would anyone give them a job in a law firm or on a sales team? Fewer than 1 in 20 history majors become college professors, and only about 1 in 10 becomes a schoolteacher. As for being underpaid, Sturtevant notes that, in the US, history graduates aged between 25 and 59 were typically earning $54,000 in 2015.[23] While your average graduate's salary is a bit higher than this ($61,000), history majors typically outearn other graduates in the humanities as well as those in education and the arts. They earn roughly the same as graduates in the life sciences (e.g. biology), behavioural sciences (e.g. psychology) and social sciences (e.g. international relations). The big bucks are earned by engineering graduates, whose median salary is over $80,000, and graduates in the physical and medical sciences typically command salaries in the mid-60,000s. However, a business major in search of riches would find they didn't earn more than the typical history graduate. Other research has shown that there's less variation between the highest- and lowest-earning graduates in the humanities than among graduates in most other fields. Even so, a quarter of history graduates in 2015 were earning upwards of $85,000.

In the UK, we can see what recent history graduates have done and how much they've earned since leaving university by looking at the income tax returns of those entering employment after graduation. This method doesn't provide information on everyone; those who work abroad or are self-employed, for instance, or who have graduated from non-English universities would not be counted. It's also worth keeping in mind that in these calculations history graduates are being lumped in with students who've got degrees in archaeology, philosophy and theology, in a category titled 'historical and philosophical studies' (H&PS for short).

It might sound a bit hokey to say that you can do anything with a history degree, but the employment figures show that this isn't far off the mark. The only sector in which no H&PS graduates could be found was 'activities of extraterritorial organizations and bodies'. They also don't appear to be outdoorsy types, since very few were plying a trade in forests, farms, fishing vessels, mines or quarries when this research was undertaken. In addition, history graduates are less likely than most other graduates of bachelor's degree programmes to go into social work, health care, construction or manufacturing.

Table 2 shows the main careers chosen by H&PS graduates in the UK. As you can see, the range of occupations is striking. The cliché that history graduates become history teachers or professors who train the next generation of history graduates just isn't borne out by these numbers. Education is a noble and rewarding profession, but H&PS graduates are only slightly keener than other graduates to choose it as a career path (13.3% versus 11.5%). They're more likely than most graduates to earn a living in the fields of finance and insurance, arts and entertainment, hotels and restaurants, public administration, and administrative and support services. More H&PS graduates become housespouses than is the norm, and they are also disproportionately drawn to 'other service activities'. Among the occupations included in this catch-all category are pavement artist, travelling knifegrinder, town crier, tattooist, poodle clipper, weighing machine operator, artists' model, clairvoyant, escort and freelance historian.

The take-home message from this wide range of jobs is that your career path will often lead you into an entirely different field from your degree subject. History students aren't like apprentice mechanics, learning a particular trade: the skills they acquire at university can be readily applied in any professional workplace. It's also unlikely that your career will progress along a single path. The typical graduate today (in any field) will change career entirely at least once over the course of their lives.

**Table 2** Industry chosen by UK graduates in H&PS entering employment, 2012/13–2016/17. Data from Higher Education Statistics Agency (https://bit.ly/39tt4IW).

| Industry | % |
| --- | --- |
| Wholesale and retail trade | 15.9 |
| Education | 13.3 |
| Professional, scientific and technical activities | 10.5 |
| Accommodation and food service activities | 8.9 |
| Financial and insurance activities | 7.2 |
| Arts, entertainment and recreation | 7.0 |
| Information and communication | 6.6 |
| Public administration and defence | 6.3 |
| Human health and social work activities | 6.3 |
| Administrative and support service activities | 6.1 |
| Other service activities | 4.0 |

The good news is that few routes are cut off by opting for a bachelor's degree in the humanities, and in history more specifically. In the US, humanities graduates who apply to law school, medical school or business school easily hold their own against other candidates. They represent roughly one-fifth of those taking the Law School Admission Test (LSAT) in order to be admitted into law school. Although smaller numbers of humanities majors apply to medical or business school, their success rates when they do are also excellent. Those with humanities degrees outperform those with business degrees on the Graduate Management Admission Test (GMAT), and only students of statistics and mathematics do better than their history counterparts on the Medical College Admission Test (MCAT).[24] UK history graduates don't have the same opportunity to enter medical school, but large numbers can and do take law conversion courses after completing their BA to become solicitors or barristers.

Because history graduates head into a variety of careers, it may take a bit longer for them to get set up than it does for those in other fields. Their lifetime earnings are good and their professional satisfaction is very real, but these can build at a somewhat leisurely pace. Even here, the data are reasonably encouraging. In the US, recent research has indicated that the return on investment for a degree from a liberal arts college outstrips that from most other universities over the course of one's career.[25]

For the UK, a snapshot of the fortunes of recent history and archaeology graduates is provided by income tax data from 2015/16.[26] The newest entrants to the job market had graduated in 2014/15. About three-quarters of history and archaeology graduates were recorded as being in gainful employment at some point in the year after graduation, which was nearly 7% below average. What's more, their median salary was initially modest at £17,900 per annum. At first glance, this may seem ominous: graduates in only half a dozen other subject areas had lower employment rates a year after completing their degrees. However, closer inspection of the statistics shows that job centres and food banks were not overburdened by down-at-heel historians and archaeologists. A small proportion (8.9%) had 'no sustained destination', and just a fraction of these would've been receiving unemployment benefits. Most history and archaeology graduates who had yet to embark on a career one year out of university were undertaking further study. This helps to explain why graduates in technology, law and the biosciences were earning no more than them at this stage.

When we turn to those who graduated in 2012/13 (i.e. three years prior to the 2015/16 tax year), we find that the average salary for history and archaeology students was £22,800. This was a few hundred pounds shy of that commanded by the typical graduate, but still ahead of that for graduates in law, some physical sciences and most subjects in the arts, humanities and social sciences. The graduating cohort of 2010/11, who had left university five years previously, were earning an average of £25,900 in 2015/16. This placed them plum in the middle of graduates from 2010/11 (the median salary being £26,000), although by this point medics, dentists and economists were all well ahead of the pack with average earnings of over £40,000.

The oldest historians and archaeologists tracked in this research were those who had graduated ten years previously, in 2005/6. A decade since completing their first degrees, their median salaries remained within an ace of those of average graduates (£30,700 compared with £30,500 overall). Male history and archaeology graduates earned more than female ones (£34,200 versus £27,800), but whether this was because of the number of hours worked, the type of occupations chosen, the impact of child-rearing or discriminatory practices is not revealed in these data. Only six subject areas produced graduates earning at least £5,000 more than the typical history and archaeology graduate after ten years. These were medicine and dentistry; economics; engineering; mathematical sciences; physics and astronomy; and architecture, building and planning. A typical degree-holder in technology, pharmacology, biosciences or veterinary sciences earned no more than £1,000 per year more than those who had graduated alongside them in history or archaeology a decade earlier.

Further evidence that UK history graduates enjoy good career prospects has been furnished by a major 2020 report by the Institute for Fiscal Studies (IFS).[27] The IFS set out to answer the fiendishly difficult question of how much extra income a student could expect to gain over a lifetime if he or she chose to go to university. This involved projecting income over the course of a career, subtracting taxes and student loan repayments, and matching graduates to non-graduates with similar backgrounds and abilities. The results therefore rest upon many assumptions, but they're nonetheless worth pondering when deciding whether to go to university and what subject to study there.

The most conservative estimate is that choosing to study history at university would add an average of £116,000 net to a man's lifetime earnings and £78,000 net to a woman's lifetime earnings at current prices. The salary boost gained by male history students ranked eleventh out of 29 subject areas. Predictably enough, their degrees were less economically valuable than those in medicine, economics, mathematics, law, engineering, business, computing, architecture, chemistry or pharmacology, and they were also just behind geography and politics. However, graduates could expect to earn more by undertaking a history degree than by studying any other humanities subject or opting for a degree in technology, psychology, most social sciences and some natural sciences, including biosciences and physics. History ranked fifteenth out of 29 subjects in its effect on lifetime earnings for female graduates. Women's different career patterns meant that degrees in education and nursing were more likely to be advantageous for them over the course of a lifetime, whereas they were less likely to gain as much economic advantage from studying architecture, technology or geography.

The evidence from both sides of the Atlantic, then, clearly demonstrates that studying history at university is a solid and sensible career decision. It may not secure you the highest possible earnings, and it could take you a bit of time to find the right kind of job, but you'll have an enviable array of well-paid career paths from which to choose.

And anyway, salaries aren't the be-all and end-all of a good job. Finding something fulfilling to do is every bit as important, and it's easier said than done. Some interesting research by Gallup in the US discovered that only 39% of college graduates are deeply involved in, enthusiastic about and committed to their work. Meanwhile, 41% of arts and humanities majors were classified as engaged; this is 4%

higher than for business graduates and 3% higher than for science graduates.[28] A different study using other measures found that 84% of workers with a BA in the humanities are satisfied with their jobs. This rises to 90% for humanities students who have gone on to receive a postgraduate qualification.[29] While these same humanities graduates were a shade less satisfied with their jobs than graduate employees overall, reporting slightly lower than average rates of satisfaction except on job location, the salient point is this: the overwhelming majority of humanities graduates like their work and earn a good wage. What's more, it doesn't follow that a worried history-inclined student who switched to a degree in aerospace engineering would be any good at it, would earn big bucks or would enjoy their every working minute. A more sensible tack is to maximize the career potential of a degree well-suited to your interests and talents.

These employment statistics lead historian Ben Schmidt to conclude that students who forsake the humanities for apparently more lucrative degrees are making a mistaken economic calculation:

*Students aren't fleeing degrees with poor job prospects. They're fleeing humanities and related fields specifically because they think they have poor job prospects. If the whole story were a market response to student debt and the Great Recession, students would have read the 2011 census report numbering psychology and communications among the fields with the lowest median earnings and fled from them. Or they would have noticed that biology majors make less than the average college graduate, and favoured the physical sciences.[30]*

It was once the case, Schmidt says, that students chose with their hearts instead of their heads and thought that education was more about 'develop[ing] a meaningful philosophy of life' than a route to 'mak[ing] more money'. He believes that one reason the humanities have fallen in popularity is that, nowadays, few students enter university prioritizing personal enlightenment over monetary gain. However, the idea that you have to choose with your head and not your heart is a false one, according to Schmidt. You can study what you love and will in all likelihood end up with a good job paying good money.

## Why choose history?

There's no denying that a working knowledge of Hannibal's exploits in the Second Punic War will seldom come in handy in the office. But the idea that history degrees are useless is based on two misapprehensions: one concerning subject matter and the other concerning skills.

The first misapprehension is that the subject knowledge acquired in other degrees is somehow supremely 'useful' in a narrowly instrumental fashion. However, this belief was not shared by a group of US business executives surveyed by Gallup. Just 11% of them wholeheartedly agreed that newly minted college graduates – from any major – are primed for the working world. The wider American public shared their doubts, with 12% fully assenting and 27% mostly assenting to the proposition that 'College graduates in this country are well-prepared for success in the workforce.'[31]

Current students were somewhat more optimistic. Around 33% were strongly of the opinion that they would graduate with the skills and knowledge required to succeed in the job market, while the remainder were broadly confident they could make their degrees work for them. Overall, they were justified in thinking they could land a job, but they exaggerated the immediate applicability of their university training. Only a quarter of graduates in work strongly agreed with both of the following statements: 'The courses you took are directly relevant to what you do at work' and 'You learned important skills during your education programme that you use in your day-to-day life.'[32]

These statistics are for graduates in general, not just history majors, who constitute fewer than 2% of all bachelor's degrees. In fact, there's not a lot of difference among graduates from all fields when asked about the direct relevance of their degrees to their jobs. Those holding BAs in business, public service and STEM fields were scarcely more likely to find themselves applying at work what they'd learned at university. There aren't all that many people who, say, land jobs as petroleum engineers after learning the nuts and bolts of petroleum engineering at university.

In truth, the US undergraduate system is designed to create generalists. Before students get to specialize, they must complete a considerable number of general education requirements designed to teach them a little about a lot. They don't get to focus completely on their chosen major until they're halfway into their degree. The major itself requires anywhere between a quarter and two-fifths of credit hours, of which a portion will be devoted to a specialized field or area. The US aims to produce well-rounded individuals, not experts in anything in particular.

In contrast, the UK undergraduate system is more specialized, at least in theory. Most UK students study fewer subjects in the last two years of school than their US counterparts are required to do in the first two years of university. The former arrive at university committed to studying one or two subjects (commonly referred to as single- or joint-honours). In practice, however, there's only so much expertise that can be accrued in a three-year degree, especially when the first year is treated by most universities as a foundation course, and by most students as a period of breaking free from school and home.

The second misapprehension is that the skills developed in history degrees aren't very practical. But what we find in reality, as careers advisor Loren Collins shows, is how directly these skills map onto the desiderata of graduate recruiters, and how closely they track the strengths discussed in the previous chapter.[33] Table 3 displays the top 15 attributes firms say they want to see in a job applicant, besides good grades, according to the latest survey by the National Association of Colleges and Employers.

**Table 3** The 15 most desirable qualities in job applicants according to US employers surveyed by the National Association of Colleges and Employers, 2018 (https://bit.ly/2VrUTwM).

| | |
|---|---|
| Communication skills (written) | 82.0% |
| Problem-solving skills | 80.9% |
| Ability to work in a team | 78.7% |
| Initiative | 74.2% |
| Analytical/quantitative skills | 71.9% |
| Strong work ethic | 70.8% |
| Communication skills (verbal) | 67.4% |
| Leadership | 67.4% |
| Detail-oriented | 59.6% |
| Technical skills related to the job | 59.6% |
| Flexibility/adaptability | 58.4% |
| Computer skills | 55.1% |
| Interpersonal skills (relates well to others) | 52.8% |
| Organizational ability | 43.8% |
| Strategic planning skills | 38.2% |

Three of the top four skills mentioned – written communication, problem-solving and initiative – encapsulate the qualities necessary to succeed as a history undergraduate. As Collins notes:

*Few disciplines on your campus will come close to demanding the kind of writing and effective argumentation that your degree requires. And because history students take responsibility for much of their own learning and research, they can approach the job market with the confidence born of genuine independence.*[34]

Moving down the list, we find other qualities that are successfully honed by history degrees. Seminars and class presentations nurture verbal communication skills. Essays demand attention to detail. The wide-ranging subject matter of the past, and the ongoing debates about its interpretation, requires flexibility and adaptability. Researching, structuring and writing a research paper and submitting it on time necessitate the kinds of organization and planning involved in any white-collar job. The depth and range of skills and abilities cultivated by history programmes, along with the value of those skills to employers, explain why history graduates do well in the job market.

## Adding value: how history students enhance their employability

Students can take several initiatives to increase their employability, building upon the strong foundation provided by their history programme. The first step is to become as articulate as possible about the skills (as distinct from the factual knowledge) you've gained by undertaking this degree. It's also wise to find ways to develop marketable skills at university that aren't necessarily part of every history programme but are often featured in newer fields in history. It's not too hard, for example, to gain some experience in quantification or computer programming. In addition, as this and other chapters will demonstrate, statistics are a powerful form of evidence, so take the opportunity to learn how to crunch some numbers. You can also enhance your teamwork and leadership abilities both within the history classroom and outside it. Often these are best evidenced through taking an active part in extra-curricular activities: swimming, debating, hiking, LARPing. It doesn't matter what you do, provided you can make a convincing case that the activity involves valuable interpersonal skills.

According to professional careers advisors who specialize in history and the humanities, there are a few practical steps you can take while at university to prepare yourself for the job market.

**Develop career goals in the first year or so of your degree.** You can get started by using online self-assessment tools, visiting your careers centre and asking friends and family what careers they envisage for you. Such fact-finding has to be accompanied by a degree of soul-searching. Staci Heidtke recommends that you ask yourself the following questions:

What are my greatest skills and interests? What's important to me about work? What have I learned from my studies? Where do I want to live? What kind of lifestyle do I envision for myself?[35]

If this seems a daunting task, Katharine Brooks's *You Majored in What? Mapping Your Path from Chaos to Career* (2009) has several useful suggestions. One method is to choose a few 'possible lives' that appeal to you from a list of jobs.[36] The aim here is not to be pragmatic or even realistic, selecting or rejecting jobs on the basis of qualifications, salary or scarcity. Instead, it's to get you to think about the common elements of your dream jobs: the activities you enjoy doing, the settings you can imagine yourself in, the kinds of people you would like to work with. Once you've ascertained your goals, Brooks recommends taking practical steps towards achieving them. Some of the typical steps along any career path are writing a cover letter, compiling a résumé, setting up a LinkedIn account, conducting internet research, contacting people in the field and acquiring qualifications and work experience.

**Gain work experience in your chosen career field.** This is a particularly smart move for students in programmes such as history, and there are several ways to achieve it. The best known is a summer internship (or an in-term internship, which more and more history programmes are encouraging). Remember, it's good practice for employers to pay interns on grounds of ethics and equality. More common in the UK than in the US is a longer work placement or 'co-op'. These placements are paid and can last for a semester or up to a year. They're overseen by the university and integrated to a greater or lesser extent into the degree programme. Larger graduate employers have formal application and recruitment processes for internships and placements, whereas smaller employers may not advertise any openings and may need to be approached directly. Many history programmes are now heavily engaged in promoting employability, so it's worth seeking help from your advisors and instructors as well as from career officers.

**Try studying abroad for a semester or a year.** Living abroad is a horizon-broadening education in and of itself, and it's all the more enriching if it cultivates foreign-language skills. It's especially valuable for undergraduates of history, as it affords them the opportunity to study the past from a different vantage point. You won't simply learn about the history of your host country, you'll also discover how differently the same trends, events and concepts are interpreted in different places. Teaching styles and modes of assessment also vary greatly from country to country, university to university. No one returns from time studying abroad unaffected by the experience; almost everyone comes back wiser, more self-confident and eminently more employable.

**Make full use of your university's careers service.** Half of US students admit to never having visited the careers service during their time as undergraduates, and under a quarter say they often avail themselves of the resources offered to them. Unfortunately, arts and humanities students are the worst offenders, with just 16% frequently using these resources, which cost substantial amounts to access off-campus. To be fair, only 22% of students who get in touch with careers officers report them as being helpful or very helpful. However, Brooks suggests that you'll only get out what you put in:

*Don't just wander in and ask if they can help you 'find a job.' Of course they can help you find a job. Be clear with them about what you want. Help them help you by setting some clear goals you would like to accomplish during your meetings with them. A better client makes a better career counsellor and results in a better session.*

Not taking advantage of the careers service is, in her experience, 'the biggest job-finding mistake most students make'.[37]

**Earn a postgraduate qualification.** Many graduates choose to take a master's or doctoral degree, whether in history or something else, although not necessarily right after graduation. In the US, over two-fifths of students who major in the humanities and the liberal arts go on to attain graduate degrees. A higher degree in any field reduces the unemployment rate among humanities graduates by a third, from 4.3% among those holding BAs to 2.9% among those with further qualifications. It increases income by a still greater measure. The median income of a history student who proceeds to gain a postgraduate degree is $80,000, 48% higher than the $54,000 earned by the average history student without a further degree, and more than any other postgraduate who majored in the humanities. The best-off quartile of postgraduates who majored in history typically earn $120,000 per year. Holders of a further degree who did their undergraduate studies in the liberal arts are more than twice as likely to find their education relevant to their career and day-to-day life as those without postgraduate qualifications. They're also more satisfied with their careers and less likely to harbour regrets about their educational choices.

⁓

The common thread in these activities is that you need to take the initiative, based on a clear understanding that a history degree is a job-relevant choice. Don't be so sure that elite universities provide all that much of an advantage. In the UK, the more selective the history programme, the less chance you'll have any mandatory employability training or modules on public history that connect the past to the present. As a student, you have to be savvy enough to realize that your degree is an essential part of your résumé but is insufficient (in most cases) to land you the job of your choice all on its own.

## What about the future?

There's one more question to address. While studying history may have been a sound economic investment in recent years, what about the fate of history graduates in the decades to come? The standard disclaimer in financial adverts that 'past performance may not be indicative of future results' applies as much to choosing degrees as it does to picking stocks. Confident forecasts of the value of any degree require the skills not of a historian but of a fortune teller. Much depends on your future actions and decisions: your performance in your first degree and any additional ones, your development of supplementary skills and experience, and your choice of career path. Other variables are beyond your control. These include the economic climate, structural changes in higher education, government policies towards student loans, and, crucially, the impact of technology and artificial intelligence on the twenty-first-century workplace.

Predictions should be treated with caution. Way back in the twentieth century, we were taught in school that automation would lead to shorter working hours and higher unemployment. Yet, the opposite has happened – at least so far. For what it's worth, the skills developed in history degrees appear to be as futureproofed as any others. Critical thinking, argumentation and communication – the stock-in-trade of any historian – accrue in value in a knowledge-based economy. So does sensitivity towards diversity, which comes from studying people in other times and places: a key feature of virtually all university history programmes today. We'll get to this in the next two chapters.

One of us works in a small programme of half a dozen historians that includes a German who teaches about China, an Englishman who teaches about Germany, an Englishwoman who teaches about America, an American who teaches about Australia and a New Zealander who teaches about Britain. Within this group is a straight historian who studies gay history, a liberal historian who studies communist history, a socialist historian who studies imperialists and a white historian who studies both slave-owners and those they enslaved. Historians might work on the past, but their interests speak to an emerging society that appreciates and negotiates cultural difference.

Our claim that studying history provides a range of very practical skills is borne out in this chapter by a variety of data on employment rates, earnings and job satisfaction. It's probable that these skills will carry on being sought after by employers well into the future. Studying history means training for adaptability, particularly in analytical skills that are readily transferable. And history students can enhance their prospects by taking some sensible steps within and alongside their history programmes.

Remember the bottom line: when you choose history, you're making a solid career move.

# PART II

## HOW HISTORY IS STRUCTURED

# CHAPTER 4

History in time and place: the common units of historical study

THIS CHAPTER AND THE NEXT offer what might be seen as road maps to historical study and research, laying out the major refinements involved in pursuing history at university level and beyond. Knowing that history programmes are often laid out chronologically and geographically, for example, will help students figure out what kinds of history they're most interested in, and what will be most relevant to their future plans. The options involved are more complicated than in school history, but they're far richer, too. In fact, having a range of choices and the opportunity to combine various categories of history are two of the defining features of a good history programme, as we shall see in Chapter 7. This variety is also part of the reason history prepares graduates for so many career options, and, more broadly, why it captures so many aspects of the human condition.

This chapter focuses on the major categories that historians most commonly use to define their work, which, in turn, help to shape university courses and undergraduate research opportunities.

**Chronology comes first.** Historians insist that the past is best understood when it's divided into major time periods.

**Geography comes next.** Historians look at various geographical units, including (but not limited to) the nation state. Interestingly, an expanded geographic scope is one of the ways in which history has changed rapidly in recent decades.

Having an active awareness of these key categories of time and place fleshes out some of the general points about historical thinking we discussed in Chapter 2, including experience with various types of change and with various layers of perspective on the present.

Exploring chronological and geographical categories in no sense traps a history student into narrow areas of concentration or selections. Nor do most students (especially in the US) need to decide what time periods and what places will be of greatest interest to them before they enter university. History programmes push students to work with a number of chronological and geographic categories, and good historians always try to make sure they're actively aware of major developments outside their own areas of specialization. However, knowing some of the commonly available options can't hurt, and since different universities offer somewhat different chronological and particularly geographical strengths, prior knowledge may in some cases help students to choose the university best suited to their interests and needs.

## Chronology

Step one in approaching college-level history involves paying attention to how time periods are defined and used. Most students have some experience with this issue from their work in school-level history, but further clarification is useful.

Many history programmes emphasize the importance of dealing with several defined time periods while making sure that students gain experience in both 'modern' and 'premodern' categories. Defining time periods matters, lest the vast amount of knowledge available in human history becomes simply unmanageable. It also matters because historians insist that developing at least an approximate grasp of the chronological order of major developments is a vital building block for historical analysis.[38] Furthermore, we all have preferences for particular periods, often for reasons we can't entirely explain. For some, it's the European Middle Ages that holds particular meaning; for others, it's classical China or colonial America.

Time periods vary, of course, with the region of the world under examination: the chronology used for China, for example, is not the same as that for Western Europe. The division between 'modern' and 'premodern' offers the most basic chronological distinction, but there are subcategories within each of these designations. Also, the boundaries of the premodern–modern divide are open to debate. For instance, some programmes see the modern period as beginning in the late eighteenth century, while others insist that students meet their 'premodern' requirement by taking at least one course dealing with developments before 1500.

More precise time periods can be identified. In many key societies, the early classical period gets a lot of attention. This can be in Greece or Rome, but also in Confucian China, early India or – though at a slightly later date – central America with the Mayan period. The Middle Ages in the West can be compared with the rise of Islam and the Arab Golden Age in the Middle East, or with vital periods of East Asian, African and American development between about the seventh and the fifteenth centuries. It should be noted that world historians are aware the 'Middle Ages' label can hardly be applied to the whole world; they sometimes use terms like 'postclassical' instead to describe the millennium after 500 CE.

For many regions, though perhaps most prominently the West, Russia and the Americas, what's known as the early modern period (which covers the late fifteenth century to the eighteenth century) plays host to a number of major developments. Some of the most significant historical moments in recent years have links to this period, such as modern consumerism (the effective origins of which have been found in the seventeenth and eighteenth centuries) and the complex relationship between China and the West, particularly with regard to developments in trade and manufacturing. In addition, recent historical analyses have added further complexity to the 'early modern' designation: it appears to be something of a swing period between agricultural and industrial forms of human activity. Expanding commerce in the early modern period, around much of the world, created environmental changes that anticipated more recent and severe shifts. The new concept of an 'industri*ous* revolution', which preceded the Industrial Revolution by developing new work patterns without much new technology, provides a window into the early modern West that also helps us to understand industrial experiences in other parts of the world in the twentieth century.[39]

While there's real debate about when the early modern period is succeeded by the modern period (sometimes termed 'late modernity'), the discussion usually centres on developments associated with the great age of Atlantic Revolutions (from the late eighteenth century to the middle of the nineteenth century) and above all the Industrial Revolution, which took shape in Britain between 1750 and 1880. The 'modern' part of this appellation can be further subdivided: into pre- and post-Civil War in the US, for instance, or into imperialism and post-imperialism in other parts of the world.

The term 'contemporary history' is commonly used to refer to the period since 1945. A Twitter survey suggested that most recent high school graduates never got around to studying this period in their US history courses because their teachers simply ran out of time before reaching the post-war years.[40] In contrast, university-level degree programmes offer explicit opportunities to explore recent decades, when the past and the present are at their most intertwined. It's hard to claim we have a full perspective on contemporary history: by definition, we don't know how the story will end when we're dealing with trends that have only emerged in the last few decades. Yet there are real skills to be acquired in analysing recent developments historically, and most college programmes offer this opportunity directly, along with their broader requirements for some chronological mix.

There's one other key point we need to make about time periods in general: they require attention, but they can also be a bit of a trap. Time periods do help historians, including history students, manage some of the distinctive features of the past and some basic patterns of change; for example, the contrast between the European Middle Ages and the Roman Empire that preceded it or the Renaissance that followed. However, some developments exceed the boundaries of particular time periods, and we need to be flexible enough to deal with these phenomena as well as the periods themselves. History students, who don't usually have to specialize too intensely, can certainly look for connections and overlap as they encounter the many chronologies in the variety of courses available to them. Defining time periods – which historians call 'periodization' – requires some flexibility.

One recent movement in particular seeks to challenge unduly narrow periodization. What its proponents call Big History (they always use capital letters, to dramatize their ambitions) urges students to develop a more sweeping sense of the human experience and its place in the physical environment. Big History begins its work well before human beings show up at all, talking about the evolution of the earth and its species as a means of encouraging a deeper sense of the human–environmental connection. Once Homo sapiens does appear, Big History focuses on some of the largest changes – from hunting and gathering to agriculture, and from agriculture to industry – rather than insisting on the more detailed periodization usually applied to the Agricultural Age. Big History isn't for everyone, but it's important for students to know about this effort. Some may even want to participate directly.

## Geography

Just as historians tend to be time-specific, they're also generally place-specific. Saying 'I'm a medievalist' or 'I'm an early modernist' captures these time period specializations. But geographical commitments – 'I'm a Russianist' or 'I'm a Latin Americanist' – run at least as deep. Furthermore, just as history programmes tend to insist on some chronological scope, they are equally, and properly, determined to make sure students avoid geographical narrowness. Thus, in the US, even the most devoted Americanist will usually be required to take at least one course that deals with some other region. The opportunity to explore many regions outside the West has been a huge boon to historical study in the past half-century.

History can offer a path towards a deeply regional specialization, sometimes in combination with other social science and humanities disciplines in area studies programmes. Whether out of personal interest or as career preparation – for example, with an eye towards diplomatic service or work in a regionally focused non-governmental organization (NGO) – students can choose history knowing it's an essential element in developing knowledge of Latin America, Africa, Southeast Asia or the Middle East.

The intensity of the area studies approach doesn't, however, constitute the most common path for history students, who tend to seek a somewhat broader historical canvas. But it's also important to note that regional choice is not the only geographical component available. Historians also tend to develop a narrower national focus within one of the major regions. A Latin Americanist, for example, is likely to specialize in Brazil, Mexico, Argentina or some other national or subregional area. European historians traditionally subdivide into national specialisms, at least during the more modern periods, which is when nation states became more prevalent. There are a few 'East Asianists' out there, but historians more commonly opt for China, Japan or Korea.

For many students, the most fundamental geographic choice centres on whether or not to specialize in their own nation's history. Some will opt to study a foreign nation or region because they want to develop wider horizons or because they feel constrained by the strong national focus of school history. Yet exploring the history of your own nation can be deeply meaningful. For many students, there's a certain urgency in figuring out why particular national patterns have emerged or how some contemporary problems or tensions have developed over time.

Career prospects may also influence your choice. Learning a foreign language as part of a history degree can expand your opportunities to work abroad. Conversely, many jobs in public history require a knowledge of national history, and history majors planning to study at law school in the US, for instance, may find a grounding in their own country's history to be advantageous.

The point is that there are choices available. As with chronology, it's really important not to be trapped. There's a tradition in some national histories to see your own country not just as an important unit for study, but as somehow special in the parade of countries around the world. In the US, this has been known to feed a sense of what's called 'American exceptionalism': a belief that the national story is not only distinctive but also measurably superior. In Britain, similar sentiments have been fostered by politicians celebrating 'Our Island Story' and making a nationalistic case for Brexit. A good history programme should offer enough geographical balance to ensure students aren't wedded to such oversimplifications.

Finally, university-level history offers alternatives to geographic narrowness that go beyond the requirement to take a course or two in more than one area. In fact, it offers two alternatives.

### World or global history

One of the really striking developments in history teaching over the past 30 years has been the emergence of serious world history programmes in various schools and many universities. In the US, the introduction of an Advanced Placement (AP) world history programme in 2001 drew the largest student audience ever for a new AP course. In Britain, the impetus towards world history has received a fillip from recent calls to counteract Eurocentrism and to 'decolonize the curriculum'.

World historians maintain that it's no longer enough for students to learn only one major tradition – for instance, Western civilization or Chinese civilization. Looking at the world as a whole is fundamentally important, and we now know enough about the histories of various key regions and the interconnections between them that some awareness of larger global patterns is both possible and desirable. Students may end up knowing a bit less about particular bits of history – for example, the Italian Renaissance – than was traditionally the case, but they'll complete their studies with an active sense of a larger framework being at play and of some of the key traditions of other major societies. Research and teaching in world history have advanced enough that undergraduate students can think of this field as a relevant framework even if they choose to specialize with a regional focus later on. Or they may opt to pursue greater depths in world history itself, taking advantage of the opportunity it presents to examine at university level the complex history of globalization.[41]

## Comparative history

The second corrective to geographic overspecialization involves attention to comparative opportunities, within or outside of a world history framework. Some caution is needed here; historians, while usually extremely place-specific, are often nervous about too much comparative work because of the concerted effort it takes to know enough about two different societies to juxtapose them accurately. This concern is legitimate, but comparative opportunities can be rewarding nonetheless. In fact, several topics offer robust comparative scholarship that will directly interest some students and serve as a model for further possible work to others. The comparative history of slavery and emancipation is one example.

Feminism, the family and labour movements have also resulted in some comparative work, and the comparative history of revolutions has an even longer pedigree.[42] More generally, keeping a comparative perspective is necessary even when working on a regional or national specialism. Any assertion of national exceptionalism, for example, is implicitly a comparative claim and deserves evaluation through genuine analysis – not just patriotic assertions. This is why in the US there are now several history programmes that seek to put American exceptionalism to the test.

## Conclusion

Historians' ability to zero in on particular times and places is vital to their understanding of specific features of the human experience. A specialization in seventeenth-century British history can allow you to have an intimate knowledge of all sorts of relationships: how civil war and political developments relate to economic and social patterns, and, in turn, how these relate to significant developments in both science and literature. This focus may be even more important when a foreign language is involved, again allowing you to grasp the many facets of a society's activity. While no history student should specialize in just eighteenth-century French history or the Han dynasty, many will take several modules or courses on a single subject in order to gain an in-depth understanding of a particular time and place.

At the same time, too much specialization can be a handicap; even professional historians must be careful not to ignore opportunities for comparison or for cross-cutting analysis across standard periodizations or regional specialities. There's a profitable tension between concentrations that improve the accuracy and manageability of historical study, and those that foster the ability to comment on broader aspects of the human experience and the nature of historical change. Good history programmes, requiring some chronological and geographic range, push students to think in terms both great and small.

Students planning to enter a university programme don't have to know their geographical or chronological preferences in advance; they'll often be able to make more informed choices after their first year of study. However, it's important to know that universities vary in their specific offerings – a point we'll take up in Chapter 6 – and that, for a few applicants, this may well factor into institutional selection. Even as you move through your university course, keeping the major categories of place and time in mind will help you to plan what sequence of courses best suits your interests.

So, geography and chronology are history's building blocks, but they can be arranged in a variety of ways. Both must be combined with the kinds of topics a student particularly wants to explore. The growing range of topical opportunities – the subject of our next chapter – may be the most exciting way to think about arranging a history programme.

*Further reading*

For more information on time periods and regionalization, see Peter Stearns's *World History: The Basics* (New York and London: Routledge, 2010). See also Robert Harms's *Africa in Global History with Sources* (New York: W. W. Norton, 2018); Robert Tombs's *The English and Their History* (New York: Knopf, 2015); and Thomas Bender's *Rethinking American History in a Global Age* (Berkeley, CA: University of California Press, 2002).

# CHAPTER 5

The history advantage: the dynamic range of historical study

HISTORY PROGRAMMES OFFER AN ARRAY of topical specialities, which are often less familiar than the chronological and geographical domains discussed in the previous chapter. Many professional historians, while comfortable with describing their area and period interests, don't claim a particular topical label. However, thematic approaches have been gaining momentum in history research and teaching alike. Some of the categories discussed in this chapter will have a familiar ring. The idea of political history as a topical focus is hardly revolutionary, for instance; most school programmes are already heavily invested in this area. But this chapter also covers some much less familiar areas, like the new thrust in digital history and the explosion of topics dealing with private life. Our aim is to present various kinds of historical targets that can help guide student choices while conveying the breadth and excitement of history today.

As this chapter will demonstrate, historians have been massively expanding the kinds of topics available for historical analysis over the past half-century. The discipline has become, once again, an engine for discovery and innovation, in terms of both the new kinds of data historians have uncovered and the types of human and social behaviour that can be explored in order to yield a meaningful past. This is where history shows its most unexpected face: in the myriad subject areas and modes of presentation that are now available. Unless a student (ill-advisedly) selects a diet of survey courses alone – world history, then some national or regional surveys – he or she will automatically encounter the richness of this aspect of historical work.

## The topical approach

This is an interesting moment to review history's range of subject matter, because there's no single 'most popular' category right now. This stands in sharp contrast to recent decades, when social and then cultural history briefly seemed to rule the roost. While history has never been tunnel-visioned as a discipline, the current dispersion is creating some interesting opportunities – not to mention a few problems.

The availability of data is a crucial precondition for any topical history exploration. The expansion of topics surveyed in this chapter has depended on major extensions to the kinds of materials historians use to conduct their research: new kinds of archives as well as new types of evidence including visual, audio, digital and artefactual. But even familiar subjects like political history are periodically invigorated by the opening up of new archives. Russian and Soviet histories, for example, were transformed in the later twentieth century by the government's willingness to bring new files to light, even before the collapse of the Soviet Union. Keeping an eye on data discoveries is an important part of comprehending history's range of current and not-so-current topics.

Surveying history's current subject matter presents something of a challenge, for there's a historical component to virtually every aspect of the human experience. In 2017, an American undergraduate, following her participation in a class discussion about the history of separate bedrooms for teenagers, put it this way:

> *I never even considered the fact that there is a history of teenage peculiarities ... I'm constantly fascinated when we observe and analyse historical changes that seem so ordinary but often are rather complex ... As I've learned, though, everything has a history.*[43]

Her statement that 'everything has a history' is truly a legitimate mantra for the discipline today; hence its adoption as a Twitter hashtag by the American Historical Association (AHA).[44]

While the fact that there's a history of almost everything is the reason historians have developed a topics list, we run the risk of encouraging an impossibly long recital of separate categories. Urban history and the history of technology, for example, are two long-established fields, each with their own journals (the mark of having 'arrived' in history) and a host of exciting findings stemming from various regions and time periods. Our education systems have their own vital histories, too. This is why most courses in education offer a basic overview of subjects such as institutional histories of gender discrimination, the replacement of largely religious schooling with state-run mass education, and sharp changes in discipline, such as the disappearance of the fabled dunce cap a century ago. The history of health, another vibrant field, includes not only the decline of epidemic disease but also the rise of new categories such as obesity, in which we can help to chart the changes and various efforts being made to confront the problem. This category also embraces the history of mental illness, including the rise and fall of psychiatric institutions. Food history is another fascinating domain that's been gaining attention in recent years. Both what and how we eat have been subject to significant changes over time. Why, for instance, has Asia taken to foods that originated in the Americas faster than Europe has, and what have been the results?

Rather than continue in this encyclopaedic fashion, what follows is an outline of 10 areas where history has staked out particularly extensive claims: some are very new, while others are traditional but with a few novel twists. These areas don't include the histories of gender and ethnicity, but not because they're less prominent. Quite the opposite: they're perspectives that are routinely applied to the history of every area under discussion. However incomplete, this list provides ample opportunity to think about history's omnipresence in human affairs and to explore the variety of its intellectual and professional implications. History's expansive range of topics applies to all of the major time periods and geographical regions, although some subject areas are better developed with regard to certain periods and places than others.

## Political and diplomatic history, with extensions

For many people, political history is the most familiar aspect of historical study, partly because it often forms the backbone of history surveys in schools. After all, every complex society was forming states from early on in the agricultural era. At the other end of the timescale, many of us spend quite a bit of time thinking about the political issues of our own day, and these cry out for some historical perspective. Between these two endpoints, many people argue that it's vital for citizens to comprehend how their nation's political system originated, how major political movements have evolved, and what some of the defining political moments in a nation's past have been. Finally, in our global world, it's important to compare national developments with those in other societies, while also examining the vital role international relations and international institutions have played in these changes.[45]

Political history comes in many forms. It can include biographies of important political figures of the past, such as the leaders of political oppositional or minority groups, as well as national heroes. It can focus on particularly formative moments, such as the English or American revolutions, or the performance of a state in a major war. It can systematically trace the evolution of major institutions – the monarchy, the office of the president or parliament, for instance. Political history takes a logical approach to the mixture of changes – in response to new ideas and new problems – and continuities that exist in political systems and values. The history of political revolutions has a rich literature of its own, which can be used to help us understand more recent upheavals such as the Arab Spring. It's important to emphasize that political history should focus not only on institutions, political parties and changing ideas, but also on the evolution of state functions in areas such as policing or education.

Diplomatic history aligns closely with political history. Here, the focus is on relationships among states: for example, what kinds of alliance systems developed in the past; how wars were resolved (and whether they offer lessons for handling conflicts today); why different periods and regions have seen different levels of conflict; and how new global institutions can help with problems like sex trafficking or climate change.[46]

A subset of diplomatic history worth mentioning is the history of peace. Peace historians deal with the changing ideas around this concept, from those held by major religions to those formed as a byproduct of optimistic Enlightenment hopes for human progress. They look at successful peace policies in the past and at the emergence of relevant international institutions in the present. Non-violence itself has a history, most recognizably in India (with leadership ranging from Ashoka Maurya to Mahatma Gandhi) but also elsewhere.

A major role of both political and diplomatic history is to provide us with examples of policies to avoid. This is a key area in which historical ignorance risks the needless repetition of past mistakes (such as McCarthyism in the US or appeasement in Britain). More tentatively, such examples may also suggest models or analogies that can usefully guide the formation of policies today, such as gun control in the US.

Another advantage of political and diplomatic history is the availability of lots of relevant source material, not only from state archives but also from a variety of protest movements. Forming useful generalizations about political change can be a challenge, and it's important to learn how to interrogate political sources for bias, but political historians are seldom short of material.

There are some problems, however, with these branches of history. For a start, they haven't been at the forefront of historical research in recent decades because many historians have been more excited about other topical approaches, as later sections in this chapter will discuss. It's unquestionably true that, until quite recently, most Western political history has involved the doings mainly of elitist white men; in reaction to this, both contemporary society and many historians have begun to gravitate towards subjects that involve greater diversity. It's also true that the importance of political history in national narratives encourages many to treat this area of study as a series of fact tests for current students. When did the Glorious Revolution occur? What was Marxism all about? These questions aren't necessarily wrong to ask – it's really useful to know this stuff – but they can make political history feel like a chore rather than an opportunity.

Both political and diplomatic history are nonetheless inescapable, even for those drawn to newer areas of historical inquiry. No exploration of African-American history or even a family history would be adequate without some knowledge of political contexts and governmental functions. This branch of history has obvious career relevance for students interested in going into law, politics or foreign service. Aspirants in these fields simply must be able to analyse historical patterns.

## Military history: an intriguing specialism

Military historians focus on war: its causes, its effects and the ways it's conducted, from leadership and strategy to technology. This field has several functions. Military history modules appeal to many students (males more than females), particularly when they focus on iconic wars. TV shows on platforms such as the History Channel deal with war more than with any other topic, offering exciting spectacle, stories of heroism and gripping tragedy.[47] Military history also serves a core instructional role for professionals, particularly in military academies. It offers lessons on the orchestration of war: old battles can provide guidance on the disposition of troops or the role of surprise in an attack. As one Command Sergeant Major put it:

*Learning from your mistakes can be a painful process. Learning from the mistakes of others is painless and easy.*

A fascinating take on a basic reason to study history.[48]

Military history offers an unusually explicit tension between change and continuity. The changes in this area can be dazzling: the introduction of war chariots, the development of new equipment for horses and new roles for the cavalry, and the advent of gunpowder all altered the face of combat dramatically. What's sometimes called the 'military revolution' of early modern Europe, which focused on changes in military organization and training as well as weaponry, is a period that garners much scrutiny. The shifting uses of naval and, more recently, air power also command a lot of attention. But continuities abound as well. The basic purpose of war – to use violence to overcome an enemy – remains constant, and some strategic options persist despite the advent of new forms of equipment. The relationship between military and civilian populations is another perennial issue. Military history also has a strong comparative element: it involves looking at the cultural and organizational characteristics of major societies, as these shape different approaches to the uses and conduct of war. It should be noted that there's been a tendency to overemphasize the Western experience in military history, but this is beginning to even out, with greater attention now being paid to other regions.

This discipline has some distinctive qualities. Professional military historians try to deal with military developments that have had a significant social or diplomatic impact, whereas amateur historians and media experts are often more taken with the details of battles, equipment and even uniforms. Military history in the services can perform a memorial function, reminding people of heroic actions or even serving in public relations campaigns. However, as we mentioned earlier, it also seeks to help contemporary leaders avoid some of the mistakes of the past. Thus, in the US, the Combat Studies Institute certifies military history trainers who de-emphasize rote-learning facts in favour of studying themes and contexts that may apply to future conflicts.

There's also an ethical dimension to military history. Those working in this field look to the Just War doctrine, which distinguishes between valid and invalid reasons for going to war. Efforts to limit the destructive effects of war often involve a serious historical dimension. Meanwhile, some popular presentations of military history, including many war films and museum displays of equipment, are periodically accused of overemphasizing the excitement and daring aspects of combat, without paying adequate attention to its human costs. Recent expansions of military history to cover the evolution of issues such as post-traumatic stress disorder (PTSD) are seeking to readjust the priorities in this complex field.

Unsurprisingly, some degree of tension surrounds the use of military history by professionals today (entertainment values for the wider public are less affected). As technologies continue to change and our focus shifts into areas such as cyberwarfare, lessons from the past may seem less important. Yet most officer training continues to find historical examples relevant, and the struggle to find solutions to new issues is forever strengthening the connection between then and now. The subject of military–civilian relations is particularly relevant, for example, in societies that depend on small professional forces rather than conscription. The changing role of women in warfare is another subject that has drawn much recent attention. The field, it seems, is gaining new vitality.

All history programmes will pay some attention to wars and military issues, but it should be noted that specialized work in military history is not always available outside of service academies. This is the kind of topical interest that can (and should) be researched in advance when students are considering different university offerings.

## Intellectual history and its outcroppings

How do big ideas get generated? How have they influenced thinkers over time and into the present? What are the roles of ideas and intellectuals in societies more generally? These are some of the central questions in this key historical field.

Intellectual history offers the opportunity to explore some of the greatest products of the human mind – but that's not all. Ideas have a history, and evaluating their development over time offers crucial insights into how societies evolve and, ultimately, how modern ideas flow from the past. While many philosophy programmes offer students the chance to learn about changes and continuities, the historical approach deals with larger patterns and the importance of connections with other components of social change.

The central concept of intellectual history is that ideas are best studied not as abstract phenomena but in terms of the historical contexts that produced them (and were affected by them) and, often, the individuals who created them. Intellectual historians also emphasize the power of great ideas, which can affect a surprising range of human activities over time. The results of this kind of historical inquiry can be truly exciting, as many students discover.

This field can take you in several directions. Many intellectual historians work on the development of particular disciplines, especially from the eighteenth century onwards. Thus, studying the trajectory of economic ideas provides us with a greater understanding of how the field of economics emerged and evolved, while also connecting it to wider historical developments. The same applies to the rich field of the history of psychology. In the UK, several programmes in intellectual history have focused on the history of political theory from classical Greece onwards. The history of ideas can also form a vital component of studies in the history of religion. Some intellectual historians are particularly interested in exploring larger movements such as the Enlightenment; here, a host of individual thinkers and a variety of specific topics can be examined, as they collectively developed major innovations with an intellectual focus.

The history of science is more or less a subfield of intellectual history, where the evolution of research and ideas about the physical universe and human anatomy is the main subject of investigation. This subfield also delves into the relationship between scientific approaches today and the practices of the past. Studying this area is one way to gain a wider appreciation of basic scientific developments amid the contemporary welter of specializations. Formal programmes in the history of science operate mainly at the graduate level – Master's or PhD – and there are several major institutions in the English-speaking world that provide them. Having said that, some teaching from these programmes does spill over into undergraduate classes, where it can at least help to spark an interest in intellectual history more generally.[49]

From the history of science came the idea of shifting paradigms, which began to generate wide interest in the 1960s. At that time, a scientist-philosopher named Thomas Kuhn argued that science is normally organized in terms of basic paradigms, which underlie basic concepts and experimental practices.[50] Periodically, however, scientists encounter problems and anomalies that these paradigms can't explain. For example, in Western science, the sixteenth century brought forward challenges to the old Greek idea that the sun rotated around the earth, ultimately generating a new (Copernican) paradigm. (For the record, several non-Western scientific traditions had cracked this already!) More recently, a similar paradigm shift occurred with the acceptance of Einstein's theory of relativity. These transitions are particularly interesting, often involving major conflict until the new paradigm becomes normalized. While this notion of a paradigm shift initially focused on science alone, it was quickly extended to other categories of intellectual activity, e.g. the history of the social sciences and psychology.

Exploring paradigms and the disruption they cause offers historians two major opportunities. First, the idea of paradigms makes it clear that basic concepts can change considerably over time, which means history is an essential part of understanding science itself. Second, and even more directly, efforts to explore and explain periods of clash and transition provide particularly fruitful opportunities for intellectual historians to contribute both to a wider understanding of the past and to an analysis of how modern ideas have emerged over time. Studying this branch of history is a deeply fascinating way of learning to deal with the phenomenon of change.

Many intellectual historians are interested not only in the origin and evolution of certain ideas but also in their dissemination. For example, a great deal of work has gone into studying the ways that Enlightenment ideas reached the wider public, including research on the history of printing and books. Similar historically informed inquiries are beginning to apply to more recent changes in knowledge dissemination, such as the rise of social media. Intellectual history has also encouraged work on intellectuals as a social group; this is a surprisingly modern development, which, again, has some interesting implications for the present day. There are obvious comparative opportunities here; for example, why do intellectuals in France seem to command greater esteem than those in the UK or the US? Studies of a related category, the intelligentsia, play an important role in Russian history.

In recent decades, intellectual historians and intellectual history programmes have been grappling with two challenges. First, as we'll discuss below, the rise of the related field of cultural history has captured some of the excitement that pure intellectual history generated in the mid-twentieth century. Cultural historians are less interested in explaining the history of key ideas than in dealing with wider popular beliefs, although the two topics are often closely related. Second, in the English-speaking world, much of the emphasis in intellectual history has long been on developments in the West, such as classical Greek philosophy, Christian theology or the seventeenth-century scientific revolution. Western innovations remain a valid area of study, but in the current global context they need to be placed within a wider framework. This involves paying greater attention to important intellectual developments in other societies (including postcolonial societies, such as India from the mid-twentieth century onwards) and giving greater acknowledgement to the ways in which Western intellectuals have borrowed ideas and techniques from other cultures. This geographical expansion has created important new avenues for intellectual history, which is currently experiencing something of a resurgence.

Opportunities to study intellectual history are available as part of many undergraduate history programmes, and they form important topical specialities. A host of intriguing issues continue to spark lively debate and discovery. Intellectual history is also appealing in terms of the accessibility of primary sources associated with it. Interpreting new ideas in science or philosophy is rarely straightforward, but the materials involved – usually written texts that are deliberately designed to present key concepts to an intellectual audience – aren't hard to obtain. Thanks to translated works, this increasingly applies to data in intellectual history outside of the Western orbit as well.

## Art(s) history

The history of the arts is a venerable field, with studies going back to at least the nineteenth century, and in some respects earlier still.[51] Important historical research opportunities are available in the areas of music, dance and theatre, although these aren't always located within the history department. And, of course, some elaborate programmes have been devoted specifically to the visual arts, such as architecture.

A variety of historians have used artistic evidence to build studies of major periods such as the Renaissance, and more recently to anchor conclusions in fields such as the history of childhood or the history of emotion (see below). However, art history is also a subject area of its own. In this discipline, historians study the evolution of major styles and genres in painting, sculpture, architecture and design. They examine individual artists and their artistic goals and training. They look at the audiences for different kinds of art, including the evolution of patronage. They study changes and continuities in patterns of art criticism. Over time, a variety of theoretical approaches have been applied to the history of art, such as Marxism and feminism as well as more purely aesthetic concepts. Increasingly advanced computer techniques are being developed to analyse various compositions, including tests for authenticity. As with other fields of history, the geography of art history has been expanding steadily, embracing Asia, Africa and Latin America as well as Western culture.

Many history students take some art history courses as part of their programme, and vice versa. But it's important to note that the study of art history is often somewhat separate from the field of history overall, and its courses are frequently located in art rather than history departments. While careers for art historians can resemble those of historians more generally, many who have earned a postgraduate degree in the former subject pursue careers as museum curators or work for art dealers and buyers.

## Social history

In the English-speaking world, social history burst onto the scene in the 1960s, and it long conveyed some of the excitement of that turbulent decade. In truth, the main principles of this field of history had been introduced earlier in France: principles that inspired and were crucial to the creation of an approach to history that deliberately, and often defiantly, challenged mainstream scholarship. Although the fervour of social history's early decades has passed, the transformation that social historians introduced in the field's heyday continues in many ways.

From the outset, social historians operated with two overlapping premises. First, they championed an approach to history that paid explicit attention to the lives and initiatives of ordinary people, not just the rich and famous. Second, they insisted that research be conducted on topics beyond politics, diplomacy and intellectual currents: topics that would better convey the issues that most people grappled with in their daily lives.[52]

Their basic points were clear as well as transformative: ordinary people have voices and histories, too, and historians can and should explore the immense variety of human experiences. These twin breakthroughs truly revolutionized what it means to study history, while linking history and historical findings to a wide array of societal concerns. In Britain, social history initially focused on class structure and on the emergence and impact of the working classes. As a result, the older, related field of labour history shifted its attention from political and trade union leadership towards the struggles of workers. The province of women's history was also a crucial early focus for social historians, paralleling the rise of second-wave feminism. As discussed, social history attended to the lives of women in general, not just a few exceptional pioneers. In the US, the rise of African-American history was an early expression of social history. So, too, was a greater show of interest in the history of immigrants and the ethnic groups from which they originated.

Social history is closely linked to economic history because of the importance of economic developments for so many segments of the population. However, as it evolved, social history began to reach well beyond economic considerations, dealing, for example, with cultural issues as well as patterns in population structure. Social historians have always debated over the balance between economic factors and value systems in defining social classes or ethnic groups, and this is an issue that remains a lively source of discussion to this day.

This aim of rescuing certain people from obscurity due to the lack of attention they've received from conventional historians – from what one social historian called 'the enormous condescension of posterity' – has been extended further still.[53] Histories of the LGBT+ community, of children and adolescents as well as the elderly, of prisoners and of the mentally ill have all become matters of intense interest. This aspect of social history can be applied to established categories such as military history; for instance, we can turn our attention towards the experiences of ordinary recruits rather than the grand strategies of generals. Interest in social groups has also broadened to include the evolution of major professions: legal history, for example, has been reshaped through greater recognition of the interaction between changing social contexts and the formation and application of the law.

How social historians approach large groups of people (as a subject) has inevitably raised some questions. How, within this field, can individuals and their roles be treated except as illustrations of larger trends? What happens to biography? There are also questions around perspective. Should social historians' focus be on the mistreatment and victimization of ordinary people or on the capacity of women or workers or slaves to create some meaning in their lives, to exert agency in wider historical processes? Questions of this sort have not been definitively resolved and continue to create some useful tensions in historical inquiry. The subordination/agency relationship also links social history directly to a variety of contemporary debates.[54]

Another revolutionary aspect of social history is the massive expansion in subjects that it's enabled historians to consider. The history of popular protest was an obvious early topic that generated some important findings about, for example, the differences between modern and premodern protest goals. Social mobility was also the subject of some fascinating research, as was family history – particularly in the US – which would soon expand into the history of sexuality. The history of crime remains an intriguing area, where historians have been able to provide both data and concepts vital to criminology in general.

More amorphous topics have emerged as well. For instance, from researching workers, social historians branched out to look at patterns of change in the experience of work itself. Leisure began to be evaluated historically, too, including society's growing dependence on a variety of professional entertainments. Sports history gained an academic following, as did the history of consumerism. Many of these topical areas invited an active exploration of changes that have continued into our own time, promoting debate about the nature – both the pros and the cons – of modern life.

Social history did more than transform history's list of topics and approaches: it led to a vast expansion of the kinds of primary sources used in historical inquiry. Everything from census documents and courtroom testimonies to private letters and diaries began to be mined for information. Social historians were also at the forefront of weighing the relative merits of quantitative and qualitative techniques. Some of them, when dealing with issues such as mobility, crime or slavery, became adept at quantitative analysis (latterly rebranded as Big Data analysis), which links the historian's toolkit to wider statistical research skills and graphic presentation. However, qualitative techniques improved as well, ultimately winning somewhat more attention.[55]

Social history was, and to some extent remains, messy. It does not necessarily produce tidy syntheses and often fits somewhere awkwardly between surveys and national histories. This can prove challenging, and some people argue that this field has weakened history's impact on the wider public by making it harder to come up with an agreed-upon national narrative (see Chapter 8 for more comments on this). Nevertheless, social history has created new opportunities for public engagement around a host of meaningful topics, from family life to ethnicity. Social history has added – and continues to add – both disruption and creativity to historical inquiry.

Over the past several decades, social history has become increasingly mainstream. There's less excited chatter about social history as a distinctive approach these days, but more of an established interest in topics such as consumerism, the African-American experience and the evolution of gender roles. While few undergraduate programmes offer an explicitly defined track in social history, almost all provide opportunities to explore a variety of social history topics. And, with social history as our inspiration, the prospects of identifying further vistas of historical research remain open. It's thanks to this area of study above all that history today involves far more than chewing over old bones.

## Cultural history

Cultural history came into its own in the 1980s, in what is frequently referred to as the 'cultural turn', although many distinguished historians had, in fact, been working in this domain since the nineteenth century. This field links to intellectual history and the history of art, but it's not focused on ideas or artistic creations for their own sake. It also resembles social history in its interest in non-elites. Cultural historians argue that one of the key ways to understand a society or group is to look at its basic values and beliefs, and the ways it expresses these. They also believe that many other facets of society follow from these foundations. Finally, they see cultural change as one of the most vital sources of innovation in human affairs, which can be traced into the present day.[56]

This field contains two related facets. The first involves an interest in popular culture directly, dealing with the evolution of voguish styles of literature, music and fashion. These are areas of rapid change in many modern societies, and studying them presents a rich opportunity to evaluate the nature and significance of new genres.[57] The second is a more anthropological approach, seeking the kinds of core values that are expressed in domains such as ritual, popular religion and gender roles. Basic work in this category has traced the decline of magic in Western society (a surprisingly recent and complex development), for example, as well as the radical notion that began to emerge in the eighteenth century that women were (or should be) more moral than men. A newer focus explores the striking increase in informality in many contemporary societies. Cultural historians argue that basic beliefs and values determine or 'construct' a variety of social features, ranging from political behaviours to emotional standards.

A wide range of topics can be evaluated through cultural history, much like social history. Attitudes towards birth and early childhood – for instance, the emergence of the modern idea that children should be happy – at one end of the lifecycle are matched by important work on the evolution of beliefs and practices around death. Focusing on changes in popular beliefs is now a dominant approach for those researching the causes of the French Revolution. Paying attention to the importance of cultural history is also a strong feature of many area studies programmes, including American Studies. The effort being made to form national value systems is a vital part of modern regional history, and it invites comparative analysis as well. A core feature of Japanese history since 1868 has centred on the nation's capacity to combine major cultural changes with important continuities from the past, resulting in a clearly modern culture that is just as clearly not from the West.

Cultural historians tend to focus on qualitative primary sources. These include what are known as prescriptive materials: edicts to guide people on how to behave as parents, spouses or teachers. The history of manners is an intriguing subfield, and it has generated some significant theories about patterns in modern societies. Several cultural historians have uncovered accounts of rituals in the past – for example, a strange massacre of cats that occurred in eighteenth-century Paris – that provide insight into popular attitudes. Changes in language can also be very revealing, such as the invention of new words, which, in turn, suggest new problems or interests. One example of this is the emergence, for the first time in English, of words like 'boredom' and 'boring' from the late eighteenth century onwards.

Cultural history has recently benefited greatly from the increasing availability of digitized texts. Digitization not only makes materials easier to access but also permits quantitative evaluations of changes in word use, which invites analysis of the causes and results of shifting cultural interests. For instance, there's been a rapid decline in references to death in the English language since the early nineteenth century. This points to changes both in the actual rates of death and in the way people were and are willing to confront the experience culturally. Students can easily use Google Ngram as a means of monitoring changes in the currency of certain words (in

English and other languages), which, in turn, can promote further analysis.

As with social history, few undergraduate history programmes offer explicit study paths in cultural history. However, most programmes offer courses that focus heavily on cultural patterns within particular chronological and geographical contexts. Given the importance of cultural issues in many societies today – in debates about cultural Americanization, racism and non-binary gender categories, for instance – there's every reason to expect that more efforts to translate the research enthusiasms of cultural history into wider classroom options are afoot.

## Public history

Public history (AKA applied history) primarily involves a reconsideration of how history is presented and how people can be trained in its presentation.[58] When the National Council on Public History was formed in the US in 1979, it sought to support the growing numbers of historians who were advancing historical findings outside of a school or university context. This group included archivists, museum professionals, preservationists, historical consultants and historians employed by the government. A similar effort arose in Britain around the same time, in the wake of the History Workshop movement. Here, the focus was on using the findings of social history, including research on the working classes, to benefit social activism and to bring additional segments of the public into historical consciousness. Interestingly, the Canadian government added 'historical researcher' as a civil service category in the 1970s as well. Even though they're not primarily academics, public historians rightly insist that they depend on rigorous historical training in order to make their findings accessible and useful to a wider audience. At the same time, public historians, more than historians in general, depend on having amazing communication skills and taking a collaborative approach to wider communities.

As public history has matured, several occupations have gained particular attention. Work in museums and historical sites (including national parks in the US) is a good example of this. The field has obviously benefited from the emergence of both cultural history and social history, which have provided new possibilities for interacting with the wider public. Often, their link to social history has helped museums to move away from antiquarianism and to give their exhibits a more active historical context.

Public history also encompasses historians who work for businesses or government agencies. They can generate publications aimed at a wider audience, but these may serve promotional or policy needs within the organization itself. A number of public historians specialize in the field of oral history, although data in this field can also be used for other kinds of recent historical research. Oral historians interview people who have participated in or observed past events. While oral history originally focused on recording the memories of important people, it's now predominantly a branch of social history concerned with the history of ordinary people and everyday life. Organizations such as the United States Holocaust Memorial Museum have tens of thousands of oral history recordings. Another American organization, StoryCorps, is actively committed to recording the stories of people from a variety of walks of life. Oral history groups are also active in Britain: one operation gathered the recollections of 1,700 veterans of World War I, while an even larger BBC project focused its collection efforts on World War II.[59]

Public history can involve interesting controversies. In Australia, its advocates have participated strongly in debates over the role and treatment of Aborigines. In the US, a major dispute erupted in 1995 over an anniversary presentation at the Smithsonian on the Enola Gay aircraft, which dropped the first atomic bomb on Japan.

Public historians had sought to include a debate over whether the bombing was justified, considering the alternative courses of action available in 1945, but pressure from many veterans' organizations and others forced the presentation to take a narrower, more patriotic approach. Disputes of this sort are unusual, but because of their wide public involvement and, often, a tradition of activism, public historians often have to deal with particular sensibilities.

As public history has developed, training at Master's (or more occasionally PhD) level has, in many countries, become increasingly common. Undergraduate tracks in public history are also readily available, including opportunities for internships. Overall, as its founders intended, the formalization of public history as a field has expanded the breadth of historical activity in many exciting ways.

## Digital history

Digital history is one of the newest and most dynamic fields within the discipline.[60] Like public history, digital history doesn't represent an expansion of the kinds of topics historians deal with so much as a new approach to existing topics. Unlike public history, however, it has major implications for the techniques used in historical research. Digital historians use computers to analyse primary sources. The first use of computers in history occurred in the 1960s and 1970s, mainly to support quantitative research in social history. Early computers could be programmed to analyse large amounts of data in fields such as demographic history, allowing changes in birth and death rates or age structures to be tracked methodically over long periods of time. Similar methods were applied to the history of protest in order to examine shifts in the size and frequency of strikes and riots. Such research continues today both in social history and, although more commonly in specialized programmes, in economic history.

Digitization eventually came to impact how sources were presented as well as analysed. In the early 1990s, pioneering digital historians such as Roy Rosenzweig in the US were beginning to produce online texts in American history that integrated images, film and sounds clips as well as text. Here was a clear indication that digitization might revolutionize the ways history was presented – both in the classroom and to the wider public – as well as researched.

Digital history often amplifies the work of public historians. A major project in Canada, for example, created a series of online presentations around the theme *Great Unsolved Mysteries in Canadian History*, which was aimed at a wide audience. Another venture titled *Los Angeles and the Problem of Urban Historical Knowledge* offered a multimedia exploration of changes in the physical profile of Los Angeles over a span of several decades. Women's history has also been embellished via digital history. *The Quilt Index* forms an online collaborative database where quilt owners can upload images and data about their quilts – artefacts that can otherwise be quite difficult to study because they're widely dispersed and often quite fragile. The outward-facing nature of digital history is signalled by the desire of its practitioners to make their work, including new programmes and tools, as widely available as possible. They're convinced that online data repositories and dynamic presentations will bring opportunities in history to a broad audience, in classrooms and beyond. There's a democratizing mission here that adds its own vigour to the contemporary history scene.

The greatest benefit of digital archives, as far as history students are concerned, is the unprecedented opportunity they present to conduct serious research on primary sources that would otherwise be too distant or too scattered for an undergraduate to access. Online archives contain multiple genres of sources and the digital tools to analyse them. One celebrated example has put all of the proceedings of the Old Bailey online, allowing anyone to explore the history of crime and law in London from the seventeenth to the twentieth century. Digital history programmes have also eagerly collected contemporary data that will be useful to historians in future, effectively amplifying what can be done through oral history. A major project collected thousands of reactions to the 9/11 terrorist attack in the US, while another explored the impact of Hurricane Katrina. Opportunities to build databases for current analysis, as part of contemporary history, as well as for later evaluation extend the reach of digital history in exciting ways.

Digital history obviously adds some important features to history courses. Most importantly, it exposes historians to training in programming and other computer-based skills. Many digital historians have thus made use of a Geographic Information System to facilitate their understanding of the spatial arrangement of social structures, touching base with an exciting new approach to geography. A project at MIT allows digital historians to present changes through dynamic timelines to help visualize time-based events. The relevant website sees this tool as 'like Google Maps for time-based information'.[61] In addition, textual analysis software supports what's called text mining, which finds patterns in masses of written evidence and thereby highlights links between digital history and cultural history. It should be noted that digital history is usually a far more collaborative discipline than conventional historical research and teaching. Teams of historians are involved in most of the major projects (often combining students and faculty members), and this can build skills beyond those applicable to technology alone.

Digital history was initially confined to several major research centres and postgraduate degrees. Nowadays, many undergraduate history programmes build some digital history into their training, with self-evident career benefits. Digital history does not displace more conventional historical skills, and it still requires the basic tools of analysis, such as assessments of change over time. However, there's no denying it constitutes a major addition to the discipline.

## Environmental history

The rise of environmental history is a testament to history's capacity to respond to changing societal needs and interests. It also demonstrates how the importance of historical perspective quickly shines through when a new issue arises. Environmental historians examine human interactions with the natural world, and both directions receive attention: patterns of change in the environment and how these affect human activities as well as shifts in our behaviour that have had an environmental impact.[62] This field began to take shape in the 1970s, in tandem with the emergence of environmentalism as a political and social movement. In the US, the American Society for Environmental History was formed in 1975. Early research focused on the history of conservation efforts of the sort that led to the national parks movement and organizations such as the Sierra Club.

Fairly quickly, however, the field broadened to include an explicit interest in patterns of environmental change and, more particularly, in environmental transformations caused by humans. A classic definitional statement thus sees environmental history as the 'interaction between human cultures and the environment in the past'.[63] This includes efforts to understand how people have thought about nature, thus linking it to cultural history, and, more recently, comparative work on engagement with environmental concerns. However, the most ambitious efforts in the field have focused on the direct evidence of environmental change. The view that human–environmental interactions are central to the historical experience has played a major role in the emergence of Big History, which we mentioned in the previous chapter.

Environmental historians devote a great deal of attention to chronicling the kinds of change ushered in by the Industrial Revolution, including regional cases of environmental degradation and the emergence of serious global environmental change. But their scope extends to other, earlier patterns as well. Thus, much attention has been paid to the impact of the rise of agriculture, and to cases where over-farming has led to significant regional developments that have directly contributed to civilizational decline. The results of colonial and imperial expansion form another topic that continues to attract researchers. The introduction of crops from other regions to feed the colonial export market often had major effects on topsoil erosion, as in the expansion of rubber plantations in Brazil. The inclusion of environmental history has also become a major theme in studies of British or Portuguese imperialism. Understanding the complex patterns of human–environmental interactions, and the efforts of societies to deal with environmental change, offers an active component for environmental inquiries more generally.

Several characteristics of the field are attached to its broad subject matter. Environmental history is highly interdisciplinary, with ties to the natural sciences in particular. The field also encourages a wide chronological frame: while studies of particular regions and moments in time are an important building block, environmental history encourages us to look at the big picture, e.g. from agriculture's beginnings to its present-day applications. The link between environmental history and advocacy is a common feature of the field as well. Historical understanding can help increase environmental awareness and promote more responsible policies.

Closely related to environmental history is another, though somewhat less developed, specialty: the history of disasters. In 1964, a major earthquake struck Alaska. One historian told us that a university's disaster research centre invited him to join their inquiry into the earthquake, so that he could provide some perspective on understanding human responses to disasters in the past. The historian had to decline because, at that point, he simply couldn't find any relevant historical work on the subject. However, over time – and thanks to this kind of stimulus – more research has emerged. A number of studies have dealt with major floods, volcanic eruptions, earthquakes, wind storms and, of course, related topics such as war and epidemic disease. The goal isn't simply to chronicle past catastrophes; it's to take a careful look at how different societies have responded to disasters or have sought to prepare for them in advance. In many cases, disaster historians seek to assess the decline of fatalism in a culture – the sense that there's nothing we can do in the face of such challenges – in favour of more productive anticipation. Not all history programmes offer an explicit focus on environmental or disaster history, but the field is growing, with important activity in both the UK and the US.

## The human experience: new historical inquiries

In recent decades, historians have been attempting to explore the human experience in several new ways while building on the achievements of cultural and social history. In 2019, for example, a university in Finland announced its ambitious new programme on the history of the human experience, offering new opportunities to deal with the relationships between individuals and wider society.[64] While this is an unusually well-defined effort, it reflects a broader drive towards understanding what people have experienced in the past and how this relates to human behaviours today.

The history of the family has been an important part of historical inquiry since the 1960s, applying to a wide array of time periods and geographical regions. Family history involves dealing with changes in family size and structure. At what points, and why, did modern societies decide to cut birth rates? What kinds of households have routinely included non-family members, and why has this practice declined? Historians have sought to understand changes and continuities in the basic purpose of family formation, including its shift from being primarily economic (in agricultural societies) to involving a wide array of emotional and consumer roles (in many modern societies). Family history intersects with legal history when examining the rates and experience of divorce. Today, with family issues being such a vital part of discussions on the quality of contemporary life, seeing the family as a changing institution means historical analysis has a key role to play in its ongoing evaluation.

Historians have also been working on the human senses, which, admittedly, isn't a topic that springs to mind when you're thinking about the relationship between past and present. A number of imaginative historians have been exploring the experience of sounds and hearing in many periods of the past, attempting to show how different this aspect of life was for civilizations gone by compared with the ear-budded society of today. A number of major works have dealt with changes in the nature of smells and the uses of our sense of smell. There are related, and fascinating, histories of perfumes and deodorants as well as of the evolution of public toilets.[65]

Sleep, too, has a history. People used to expect different patterns of sleep and wakefulness from the standards urged by societies today. Opportunities to nap have changed over time. Sleep, in fact, has probably become more difficult in modern societies than it once was: a statement that presents yet another opportunity to both explore historical differences and use history to shape the ongoing evaluations of our own time.[66]

The history of emotion has also become a major subfield. The basic concept behind the history of emotion is simple enough: emotions combine biological experiences with cognitive appraisals, which, in turn, are strongly conditioned by cultural standards. These standards can and do change over time.[67] Thus, happiness has a history, as we have seen in Chapter 2. One of us wrote a book about how expectations of love have evolved over time.[68] The other has written extensively about the history of emotions, such as about how shame has been redefined. Older practices of shaming, such as putting people in public stocks for offences against community morality, seem bizarre to us. Yet the history of shame underlies some major issues in society today.[69]

Efforts to delve more deeply into the human experience are still a historical frontier. They raise important questions about how to find relevant information and how to deal with the relationship between recommended behaviours and actual emotional or sensory life. Further exploration remains essential. It's a field that encourages the use of history as a way to evaluate current issues, both by showing how these issues contrast with the past and by dealing with the kinds of change that have led to our behavioural patterns today. Asking ourselves 'What's the history of that?' opens up new facets of the past and offers fresh perspectives on the present.

## Navigating history's paths

History today faces two challenges that directly relate to the variety of topics historians are currently exploring, and students considering history should be aware of both: the first is coherence and the second is audience.

The current proliferation of topics and our interest in constructing valid and vigorous pasts for many different social groups and aspects of human life have undeniably made it harder to identify a single historical narrative than it once was. It was easier to define what needed to be known about national history when the focus rested primarily on politics with a bit of economic and intellectual history thrown in. There's no question that crafting even the simplest kind of coherence is more difficult today because we know so much more about the past. Whether this is a problem or not may be debated, and students should think about the issues involved. This is decidedly not your grandparents' history programme.

The issue of audience is a more obvious challenge. Many academic historians talk mainly to each other and, of course, to students. This is no truer in history than in most other disciplines, but it's possibly more the case now than it was in previous decades due to the fragmentation of our discipline into so many specialities and sub-disciplines. Major historical findings are (or should be) a matter of real public interest, as they bear directly on contemporary issues in politics, global relations and personal life. They can also contribute to a variety of policy discussions. Yet addressing this wider audience is not easy. Students can usefully be aware of the challenge here, and some may turn out to be interested in exploring it explicitly. Programmes in public history and the histories of gender, ethnicity, sexuality and the environment offer new ways to reach out, and this is a key reason that interest in these areas has been growing. The opportunities presented by digital history have also been a factor. That there's a gap between history's potential and its public perception is undeniable, but this doesn't have to be permanent: it's just another opportunity for student creativity.

Our crucial point – the extent to which history has changed and expanded over the past several decades – remains. While maintaining its traditional strongholds in areas such as politics and the military, the discipline has extended, data permitting, to encompass the whole chronology of the human experience. Its geographical range has become global. Its topical range has been revolutionized several times over. These changes position history to contribute actively to our understanding of this now-global world, and to help address its many issues, from diversity to climate change.

The array of topics history now deals with offers a lifetime of learning, whether one becomes a professional historian or simply maintains an active interest in this field while pursuing another career. There's always a new subject, a novel opportunity to combine history with the findings of some other discipline, a chance to think about the connections between past and present in fresh ways. History offers abundant and ongoing intellectual stimulation, and that's a treat in itself. By making choices about how best to take advantage of the expansion of history's domain, students can advance their own process of exploration.

The variety of major historical topics available, in addition to the more familiar list of basic time periods and geographic regions, makes for a dynamic discipline that's working to expand knowledge and to link history to fundamental contemporary issues. A history student is not expected to commit to a topical specialism when entering university. It's quite sensible (and often a requirement) to take a variety of history courses at the start of an undergraduate degree before choosing a particular path. If, however, you have a glimmer of a particular interest, this can help to guide your selection of a history programme. All good history programmes will offer you choices, and almost all will offer strengths in established fields such as political, cultural, social or intellectual history. Strengths in more specific areas vary from programme to programme. It's also worth bearing in mind that history programmes in slightly less well-known institutions have sometimes been particularly ambitious in creating new options. This was true of social history in the past, and it certainly applies to public and digital history today. These cutting-edge fields offer exceptional opportunities for research projects and internships to interested undergraduates.

Most history programmes are designed to give students the chance to take courses in other areas, and a variety of topics promote a number of connections. Having the opportunity to pursue related interests is one of the key differences between history and many STEM programmes, where curricula are more tightly regimented and there's less student choice. Of course, historians are delighted when a student wants to take more history courses than required, but, in our more responsible moments, we do advise students to come up with imaginative combinations of modules on their own (including relevant minors for those studying in the US). Many opportunities follow from history's own expanding topical range. Thus, students of digital history might pursue further work in computer science, while those focused on cultural history could turn their attention to literature and anthropology. Anyone exploring the history of the family or emotions can cross-link their studies with sociology and social psychology.

Again, there are no prescriptions here, and there's certainly no need for a full multi-year plan when entering university. It's just helpful to be aware of history's many options and how they relate to a wide range of collaborations in building an exciting undergraduate programme. It's also important to learn how to deal with interdisciplinary challenges. Choosing a history programme that caters to these and other interests is the subject of our section.

# PART III

STUDYING HISTORY AT COLLEGE
AND UNIVERSITY

# CHAPTER 6

Evaluating history programmes

THIS BOOK IS DESIGNED TO help you decide not only whether to study history at university but also how to get the most out of a history major or degree. One of life's little jokes is that it places one of the most difficult and consequential decisions at the very beginning of adulthood. Studying at university will be your life for a few years and will affect you for decades after that. What you study, and where you study it, will shape the kind of person you become. All sorts of factors affect your choice of college or university, and there's no reason to ignore considerations such as location, size, extracurricular glitter and so on. Students must also calculate their chance of admission to a given university and, in the US, how its tuition fees compare with those in other institutions. For a student interested in history, there's every reason to add some evaluation of relevant academic programmes to the list. This chapter seeks to assist you with that process.

Choosing a degree programme at a university or college is also one of the most significant financial decisions you'll ever have to make. It's an investment of a kind, where the cost of the loans and expenses you incur must be weighed against the potential benefits of securing a lucrative career on the strength of your degree. The difficulty isn't just that you're expected to make such an important investment decision as a young person: it's also that it's incredibly hard to make an informed choice. Imagine that choosing your university and degree subject is equivalent to choosing a particular make and model of car to purchase. Your first problem is the range of options. There are a couple of hundred car manufacturers (that is, universities) in the UK, and several thousand in the US. Each manufacturer has its own make of degree that comes in many different models (AKA majors or degree subjects). These often run into the hundreds. Multiply the number of makes by the number of models and you'll find yourself with tens of thousands of possible degrees to choose from.

At first sight, it appears that each manufacturer is offering a similar range of models (including, in most cases, a history degree), but on closer inspection you'll find that every model is a unique product. No two models contain exactly the same components, even if they're called the same thing. Now, you want to buy a car that will reliably allow you to reach a particular destination: a good degree, a good job, a fulfilled and happy adult life. Unfortunately, it's not always clear in what direction you need to travel to reach that destination, or which cars are equipped for the journey. Some cars will give you a smooth ride; others might be unsuitable for the particular road you have in mind.

It's hard to decide which car to buy for a number of reasons. Variation in price is a major consideration in the US. Another is that, in this particular analogy, you've never driven a car before. What's more, it's not really possible to take this kind of car for a test drive. The manufacturers encourage you to visit their showrooms (on campus or online) but, like stereotypical car salespeople, they're unlikely to give you a fully objective view of their products. You can also ask existing car owners what they recommend. The problem here is that they've purchased a single make and model of car (often decades ago), which may be quite different from the type you have in mind.

If you somehow overcome all of these obstacles and pick the car you believe is right for you, there's one last potential difficulty: the manufacturers might well refuse to sell it to you. Some prestigious makes and models come in limited editions that are only available to a select few. You won't know whether or not you can buy any particular car, however, unless you're prepared to put down a non-refundable deposit by paying an application fee in the US or using up one of the five options on your Universities and Colleges Admissions Service (UCAS) form in the UK. If you put down this deposit, the manufacturers agree to sell and you can meet their price by fulfilling the entrance requirements, only then do you get to kick the wheels, buy your car and hit the road.

Of course, degrees aren't cars, and studying is much more than a simple commercial transaction. Many academics (the authors included) reject the commodification of higher education underlying this comparison, but our point is that you have to make a big decision based on limited solid information. It would be nice to think that everyone ends up happy with their decision: nice, but wrong. In the UK, a third of all undergraduates wish they'd done a different degree, had gone to a different university or hadn't gone to university in the first place.[70] This buyer's remorse is even more startling among US adults who completed their education with a bachelor's degree. Out of those who took part in a 2017 Gallup survey, two-fifths said that, given their time again, they'd have studied a different major, and a quarter said they'd have attended a different institution.[71]

If this book helps one person to make a better choice of university and degree subject, then it'll have been worth the writing. This is, we admit, exactly the kind of emotionally manipulative line that you might expect from two car dealers like us. It's true that both authors have been in the history trade for many years, and we've devoted our lives to teaching and writing about the past. That said, we're not working on commission. Whether or not you decide to study history, what kind of history you study and where you study it will affect your life, not ours. What's more, as historians, we treat evidence with care and respect, much as medical doctors treat patients in accordance with the Hippocratic Oath. Our job in this book is to provide you with the evidence that will enable you to make the best decision for yourself.

## Investing in education

First, a no-brainer. If you have the chance to study at university, do so. It's not essential to have a degree, but not possessing one is like being car-less in rural Montana or the Scottish Highlands. Being degree-less will, in all probability, limit your opportunities and make day-to-day life more of a struggle. To be sure, studying at university involves costs as well as benefits. On both sides of the Atlantic, there are justifiable concerns about the price of higher education. In England, students justifiably baulk at the flat-rate annual tuition fee of £9,250 levied on virtually every degree course. This is roughly the same amount as US students pay for in-state tuition at four-year public institutions ($10,230), but much less than the average fees at out-of-state public universities ($26,290) or non-profit four-year private colleges. In fact, the tuition cost of an entire undergraduate degree for English students (approximately $36,000) would cover only a single year of tuition at a typical private university in the US ($35,830).

There are all sorts of reasons for dissatisfaction over current tuition fees. The declining public support for higher education in both the US and the UK has contributed greatly to rising costs. Furthermore, universities carry out a significant number of functions besides teaching, which are funded in large part by tuition fees. History students, who are relatively cheap to teach, shoulder a disproportionate amount of the burden. Yet a university education remains one of the best investments you could ever make. The average salary of an American with a high school diploma is $36,000; that of someone with a bachelor's degree is $61,000. Once you're at university, it's important to get at least a BA. Taking some college courses or leaving with a two-year associate's degree will only bump up your salary by $6,000, on average, over that of high school graduates. As discussed in Chapter 3, it's advantageous to obtain a further degree in addition to a baccalaureate. But we're jumping the gun a little. You can't get a Master's degree without first getting a bachelor's degree, and if you don't get a bachelor's degree, you could end up paying a heavy financial cost for the rest of your life that far outweighs tuition fees, however extortionate they may appear at the time. Most people are well aware of the 'graduate premium'. In a 2015 Gallup poll, 70% of Americans strongly agreed that a degree was necessary to secure a good job. The same proportion (70%) believed that higher education will become still more important to employment prospects in the future.[72]

## Degrees and institutions

So, step one is to attend university if at all possible. But which university, and which subject? Even if your heart's set on studying history, this only reduces the choice to approximately 100 universities in the UK and nearly 1,300 universities in the US. Applicants to UK universities have to narrow down their choices pretty fast, as they can only apply to a maximum of five specified degree programmes. These five are then whittled down to two: their 'firm' first-choice programme and an 'insurance' choice if they don't achieve the exam results required by their first-choice university. For most UK students, the decision whether or not to study history therefore takes place in their last year at school.

In the US, however, you can apply to as many universities as you like, provided you're willing to pay an application fee to each one. Furthermore, you apply to study at the university rather than (as in Britain) to study a particular degree in a particular department at a particular university. Most US universities invite you to specify your intended major, but no one will hold you to this; one survey suggests that half of those who enter university are undecided on the matter. You need only declare your major in your sophomore or junior year, and you can change your mind thereafter. A total of seven in 10 students in the same survey switched their major at least once (and often more than once) during their undergraduate studies.[73] As a result, the offerings of specific degree programmes barely feature among the main reasons why US students say they chose to study at one university over another. Instead, this list is dominated by practical considerations, such as location, cost, selectivity and reputation, both as a place to study and as a launch pad for future employment (see Table 4).

**Table 4** Reasons listed by US undergraduates for choosing a specific university. *Source:* Strada Education Network and Gallup, *Why Higher Ed? Top Reasons U.S. Consumers Choose Their Educational Pathways* (Washington, DC: Gallup, 2018), p. 9.

| | |
|---|---|
| Location | 28% |
| Access/affordability | 22% |
| School reputation and fit | 20% |
| Good job or career | 19% |
| Learning and knowledge | 5% |
| Family or social expectations | 4% |
| Other | 1% |

It's nevertheless worth asking at the outset whether the type of university you go to will affect the kind of history you're likely to study. Answering this question isn't simple. It requires

► finding out what modules are offered or what specialisms are advertised at each university,

► coding this information so that it can be compared with that of every other university, and

► poring over the results to identify similarities and differences between types of university.

To save you the trouble of several months' investigation and analysis, we have done this job for you. Lots of useful information is available on the chronological periods and geographical regions history programmes cover (corresponding to our discussion in Chapter 4), and while topical strengths are less easily categorized, we offer some information on that score as well (see Chapter 5). These findings can help students to decide where, as well as what, to study.

Students who are thinking about progressing in history should know something about major institutional types, but they might wish to go beyond this. Catalogues can be invaluable here, once a small number of possible institutions have been identified. However, there are some other steps to take first, in terms of organizing available data and criteria. Here, for clarity's sake, we proceed separately for North America and for the UK.

## Studying history in North America

Let's start with North America, where we'll look at the different types of universities and colleges, the range of geographical and chronological coverage, and, finally, topical specializations. The system generally used to categorize universities and colleges in North America reflects the size and complexity of its higher education system. While UK universities can be meaningfully divided into three groups, US universities are organized via the Carnegie Classification of Institutions of Higher Education into no fewer than 33 basic categories. For our purposes, these can be boiled down to five (R1, R2, D/PU, MA and UG), plus a sixth category of Canadian universities. The first three categories (R1, R2 and D/PU) all designate research-intensive universities. As the name suggests, Master's Colleges and Universities (MA) grant Master's degrees but not doctorates. Then there are Baccalaureate Colleges (which grant nothing higher than four-year bachelor's degrees), Associates Colleges (which grant associate's degrees, which are equivalent to the first half of a BA) and an array of Special Focus Institutions. These undergraduate-focused institutions are highly diverse, ranging from highly selective (and expensive) liberal arts colleges to community colleges that are inexpensive and open to all comers. These are nonetheless grouped together in this analysis under the category UG.

The nature of particular history programmes reflects these institutional categories to some extent, but there are some surprises. This becomes evident when we map our six categories against the 'areas of specialization' provided by 650 North American history departments for the American Historical Association's *Directory of History Departments and Organizations* (AHA Directory for short). A typical department uses five or six terms to describe itself, which is not a lot considering that a typical department will employ roughly 30 faculty, each of whom will have highly specialized expertise.

To find out who specializes in what, we classified each term appearing in the AHA Directory by period, place and theme. For example, 'colonial New England' is listed by Austin Peay State University as one of its areas of specialization. This term was classified by period as early modern and by place as North American, but it couldn't be classified by theme. Since Austin Peay is a Master's University, these classifications were added to the figures for those universities also in the MA category, so that their areas of specialization could be compared with those of universities in other categories. Additional information provided in the AHA Directory about the number of faculty and students at each university was also added into the mix.

These staff and student numbers are a good place to start, with US history programmes being roughly divided into four sizes. About a quarter of North American universities have over 200 students majoring in history. Arizona State University has over 1,000. Four other large state universities have more than 500 history majors (University of California, Los Angeles (UCLA); University of Texas at Austin; Colorado State University; and California State University,

Long Beach), as do four Canadian universities (McGill, Concordia, Toronto and York). Next up, a quarter of universities have between 100 and 199 history majors. Another quarter have between 50 and 99 history majors, and a final quarter have under 50 history majors. The 31 universities with 20 or fewer history majors range from Chestnut Hill College to the California Institute of Technology (Caltech).

With notable exceptions such as Caltech, the smaller history programmes tend to be based in the MA and UG universities. Small can often be beautiful, according to a Gallup survey of current undergraduates in all disciplines. Those studying at universities or colleges with under 5,000 students were almost twice as likely to state that their instructors cared about them as people. Students at smaller institutions were also more likely to have found a mentor and a tutor who made them 'excited about learning'. There was less of a difference in the proportion of students at smaller and larger institutions who were highly active in extracurricular activities, who had an internship or job relevant to their studies, or who undertook long-term research projects; however, in every case, smaller institutions had the edge over larger ones.[74]

If you expected the number of history faculty to be related to the number of history majors, you'd largely be correct. There's a 0.66 correlation between the two figures, and two of the half-dozen universities that list over 100 faculty (UCLA and Toronto) have more than 500 history majors. So, how do we explain that New York University (NYU) and the University of Michigan, Ann Arbor also employ over 100 historians but have 314 and 273 history majors respectively? A clue lies in the fact that these two universities list roughly one postgraduate for every two undergraduates. So it's not that undergraduates at NYU and Michigan are being assigned a professor each or are taking classes containing only a handful of students. In reality, the focus of the faculty at universities such as these is less likely to be on teaching undergraduates than on supervising doctoral students and conducting their own research. However, the greater range of specializations offered by these big research institutions may be attractive to some history majors.

When we look at the different 'areas of specialization', the first thing that jumps out is that US history programmes don't seem to be all that different from one another. For example, Whitman College in Walla Walla, WA lists as its specialisms Africa, Europe, the US, East Asia, Latin America, the Islamic world, the ancient Mediterranean and environmental history. Whitman is justifiably proud to 'offer a curriculum that is incredibly diverse for a school of our size', but these classifications are little different from those provided by Princeton University, which has more than six times Whitman's number of historians on its staff.[75]

**Table 5** North American colleges and universities by type, listing places as areas of specialization, 2019. Based on data from the AHA Directory.

| Uni. type | North & Central America | South America | Eur. | Asia | Africa | Oceania | Global |
|---|---|---|---|---|---|---|---|
| R1 | 91.5 | 61.2 | 83.7 | 57.4 | 48.8 | 3.9 | 18.6 |
| R2 | 96.9 | 42.3 | 83.5 | 36.1 | 40.2 | 1.0 | 28.9 |
| D/PU | 94.4 | 51.9 | 90.7 | 57.4 | 42.6 | 5.6 | 22.2 |
| UG | 97.0 | 62.4 | 93.2 | 77.4 | 58.6 | 5.3 | 15.0 |
| MA | 98.6 | 52.7 | 90.8 | 63.3 | 48.8 | 5.8 | 25.1 |
| Canada | 96.7 | 53.3 | 80.0 | 50.0 | 46.7 | 3.3 | 16.7 |
| All | 96.2 | 54.8 | 88.3 | 59.8 | 48.9 | 4.5 | 21.7 |

In a sense, however, that's the point. North American history departments generally see it as their responsibility to remain unspecialized: to teach as large an expanse of time and space as they possibly can. This desire to cover as many bases as possible has created some issues in the current climate of political partisanship. Those on the left sometimes accuse history departments of privileging the voices of dead white European males. Those on the right tender the opposite allegation: that tenured radicals indoctrinate students, and that too much attention is paid to social history and the experience of minority groups or non-Western regions.[76] Most historians would counter that they are trying to offer a broad range of perspectives and to adjust their programmes to fit the changing contours of the modern world.

**Table 6** North American colleges and universities by type, listing time periods as areas of specialization, 2019. Based on data from the AHA Directory.

| University type | Ancient | Medieval | Early modern | Late modern |
|---|---|---|---|---|
| R1 | 14.7 | 20.2 | 23.3 | 36.4 |
| R2 | 8.2 | 14.4 | 15.5 | 28.9 |
| D/PU | 9.3 | 7.4 | 13.0 | 31.5 |
| UG | 15.0 | 13.5 | 12.0 | 24.8 |
| MA | 14.5 | 17.4 | 13.5 | 36.2 |
| Canada | 10.0 | 20.0 | 20.0 | 33.3 |
| All | 13.1 | 16.0 | 15.7 | 32.3 |

In fact, the predominant areas of specialization listed by history departments would satisfy neither the left nor the right, which might be another way of saying that most departments seek to balance contending claims. Europe comes in a close second to North America in terms of mentions, but just one university in seven lists *only* North America and/or Europe among its specialisms, and a mere three institutions are Eurocentric enough to list Europe as the only continent in which they specialize. The fact that over half of departments list a specialism in Asia or in South America, and almost half list a specialism in Africa, shows that departments have broadened their horizons considerably over the last generation. The expansion of non-Western and Southern Hemisphere history in North American universities may have happened too quickly for traditionalists and too slowly for progressives, but it's a change of immense significance. R2 universities appear to be the slowest at making the change, however, with this category possessing the lowest number of specialisms in Asia, Africa or South America. UG universities, conversely, mention these three continents the most. The higher proportion of R2 universities that specialize in world history does not fully offset their relatively limited global reach.

The figures for period coverage are harder to interpret. The fourfold categorization of ancient, medieval, early modern and modern is also of limited applicability outside Europe, where it originated. Moreover, universities are less likely to describe their specializations in terms of time than in terms of geographical coverage. R1 universities are more likely to include time spans, which shows that the larger, more research-intensive universities are better equipped to teach the full sweep of history from ancient times to the present day. Although there's more mention of late modern specializations in every type of university, modern history appears to be less dominant in R1 and also Canadian universities, which tend to have large, research-intensive history faculties. The further back in time you go, the fewer areas of specialization are mentioned. There are twice as many late modern areas of specialization listed as early modern ones. Early modern specializations outnumber medieval ones, which, in turn, outnumber specializations in ancient history. It's worth noting, however, that the British custom of hiving off ancient history into separate classics departments is less common in the US, creating greater opportunities for US history students to study the earliest historical periods within their own programme.

**Table 7** Themes listed as areas of specialization by history programmes at North American universities, 2019. Based on data from AHA Directory.

| Areas of specialization | Number of universities | % of universities specifying theme |
|---|---|---|
| Ethnicity | 115 | 29.0 |
| Public | 110 | 27.7 |
| Gender/sexuality | 105 | 26.4 |
| Social | 101 | 25.4 |
| International/comparative | 98 | 24.7 |
| Cultural | 98 | 24.7 |
| Military | 79 | 19.9 |
| Science/medicine/technology | 67 | 16.9 |
| Environmental | 53 | 13.4 |
| Political | 46 | 11.6 |
| Other disciplines | 38 | 9.6 |
| Methods/skills | 24 | 6.0 |
| Economic | 15 | 3.8 |
| Miscellaneous | 8 | 2.0 |
| Total specifying themes | 397 | 100.0 |

Some broad trends can be identified in the topical specializations listed in the AHA Directory. Three-fifths of universities (397 of 650) listed one or more thematic topics among their specializations. Ethnicity received the most mentions, with gender and sexuality coming in third – a sign that history's expanding beyond its traditional focus on 'the pale and the male'. It's striking that topics such as economic and political history appear towards the bottom of the list. Yet equally traditional subjects such as military history and the history of international relations can be found in the top half of the table. Both social and cultural history also crop up frequently, but these are less intimately connected to identity politics than the histories of gender and ethnicity. The prominence of public history helps to dispel the misapprehension that history is a willfully irrelevant subject.

The categories we can evaluate for North American institutions leave out at least one important element that will appear in the programme requirements listed in each university's course catalogue. Almost all history degrees require some work on research methods and the nature of historical thinking or historiography. In addition, the majority encourage, and in some cases require, students to take part in research projects in some form of capstone experience. These are also factors to keep in mind both when deciding whether to progress in history and when evaluating programmes at different universities and colleges.

## Studying history in Britain

When we turn to what's taught where in British universities, we discover that there's no such thing as an average history degree. In this case, the authors have classified all core (compulsory) modules taught at every UK university that offers a single-honours history degree. To return to the car analogy, each 'make' of the history 'model' of degree has its own unique selling points. The differences between history degrees are nonetheless not entirely down to the hobby horses and bugbears of the history faculty at each university. On the contrary, what is included and excluded from history degrees is a largely pragmatic matter. Any conception by staff of what a history degree ought to be has to be reconciled by practical considerations about the resources at their disposal and the needs and wants of students, university managers and other stakeholders.

In practice, this means that, amid the myriad variations among history degrees, it's possible to identify three main types of history degree corresponding to the type of university at which they're taught. Like most things in Britain, universities are riven by hierarchy and status-consciousness. Two dozen universities belong to the Russell Group, which regards itself as representing the most 'research-intensive' institutions and is commonly regarded by the general public as a byword for academic excellence. There are twice the number of history degree programmes (48 of them) at 'New' or 'post-1992' universities. What was new in 1992 was that these institutions were converted from polytechnics to universities. This was intended to remove the quintessentially British stigma towards practical and vocational education, but it remains the case that these universities are viewed as either less elitist or non-elite, depending on your standpoint. A further 30 history degrees are taught at universities that aren't ex-polytechnics and haven't been admitted to the self-selecting Russell Group. There's no agreed name for this third category, so we'll term it 'pre-1992' universities.

Contrary to their exclusive reputation, history degree programmes at Russell Group universities tend to enrol large numbers of students. In 2015, there were four times as many students enrolled in history at your average Russell Group university as at your average New university. Russell Group undergraduate history programmes were well over twice the size of those at pre-1992 universities, too. The number of history staff at each type of university conformed to those same proportions. For every historian at a typical New university, there were two at a typical pre-1992 university and four at a typical Russell Group university. If value for money is measured by contact hours, then New universities offer the best deal. They provide their students with a third more classroom time than either Russell Group or pre-1992 universities. New universities also assess their students differently, with exams accounting for just a sixth of their assessments. In comparison, exams represent a third of assessments at pre-1992 universities and two-fifths of assessments at Russell Group universities. Since written comments are much more common for coursework than for exams, students at New universities can expect to receive more feedback as well as more teaching.

The structure of a typical history degree programme differs in significant respects in the three types of university. If you choose to study at a New university, you would take an average of eight core (that is, compulsory) modules. This means that roughly half of the modules taken by history students in New universities are selected for them, with the other half being chosen by students from a list of options. Four of the compulsory modules will typically be periodized, which means they cover a specified time span. Of these, three will be partly or fully located in the late modern period (since 1800). There's a good chance that one module will deal to some extent with ancient or medieval history, but it's unlikely that it will be exclusively so. In terms of area coverage, these four periodized modules will probably include one British, one European and one world or imperial history module. The fourth periodized module could be another one on British or European history, or it might be on World War I or World War II, or on American history or the Atlantic World (i.e. the triangular relationship between Europe, Africa and the Americas). It might also be a thematic module that isn't place-specific. New universities generally require a module on historical methods, one that combines skills with historiography (that is, historical theory and the development of history as a discipline), a dissertation and one more core module. This could be an employability module, something on local or public history, or one of the other topical specialities described in Chapter 5.

A typical history degree at a Russell Group university differs in significant respects. Two fewer core modules, generally periodized ones, are taught as part of your average Russell Group degree. One of the two remaining periodized modules is likely to include coverage of the late modern period and the other isn't. Despite Russell Group universities requiring only half as many periodized modules as New universities, students at both types of university receive the same (small) amount of compulsory ancient and medieval history. Russell Group history students are less likely to be required to study Britain or the Americas, imperial history or the Atlantic World. Some will be asked to choose from a range of modules on a specified period, providing a degree of optionality within their programme requirements. Students in both Russell Group and New universities will probably take a module in skills and methods and a module including historiography. Russell Group universities are more likely to teach historiography as a stand-alone subject. Russell Group students might also be required to complete a research project, a group project, a module on public history or an 'interdisciplinary' module that considers history alongside other subjects in the humanities or social sciences. They're much less likely to be required to take modules on local history or employability.

Between New and Russell Group universities are the 30 pre-1992 universities that are neither fish nor fowl. Their history degrees combine elements found in those of the other two types of university. They resemble Russell Group universities in that they offer a similar number of core modules and a similarly modest number of contact hours. The proportion of assessment by examination is lower than in Russell Group universities, but it's still twice that of New universities. However, the pre-1992 universities are more similar to New institutions regarding programme size. Like New universities, half of their core modules are periodized, and these are just as much weighted towards the late modern period. They probably include a module apiece on Europe and world or imperial history. The other periodized module is less likely to be about Britain than in New universities. A dissertation, a historiography module and a combined historiography and methods module are commonplace in the pre-1992 group of universities as well.

**Table 8** Characteristics of UK history programmes by type of university, 2015. *Source:* Higher Education Statistics Agency.

| Characteristics | Russell Group | Pre-1992 | New | All |
|---|---|---|---|---|
| Number of universities by type | 23 | 33 | 50 | 106 |
| Average number of staff | 49.0 | 21.8 | 11.7 | 22.9 |
| Average student intake | 319.3 | 119.4 | 80.5 | 144.4 |
| Average number of compulsory modules | 6.1 | 6.1 | 7.7 | 6.8 |
| Average number of compulsory survey modules | 2.1 | 1.8 | 2.8 | 2.4 |
| Average percentage of study time spent in classes or placements | 14.9 | 15.1 | 20.6 | 17.6 |
| Average percentage of assessments as exams | 40.9 | 31.1 | 16.7 | 26.4 |

## From data to decisions

This chapter has offered up lots of information about the similarities and differences between history programmes at various types of institution. Even when armed with this battery of information, choosing what to study and where to study it remains difficult. For most students, the range of options within the degree is, and should be, less important than other factors including cost and accessibility. When one of the authors served as an admissions officer, the first piece of advice he would offer to prospective students was to consider the kind of place they preferred to live. Some people thrive in big cities; others prefer the communal atmosphere of a small-town campus university. The size of the institution also matters. Again, there's a trade-off between the greater resources available in a larger institution and the stronger networks and support structures that are likely to exist in a smaller one.

When assessing history programmes, you'll need to put all your powers of critical analysis to use.

**Get in touch with current students** and, where practicable, visit the campus and attend talks and sample classes.

**Think hard about the representativeness of the evidence.** Don't be too swayed by the opinion of a single student or a star turn by an engaging instructor. Go beyond what the programmes want to show you in order to discover what you actually need to know.

If you'd love to study abroad, make sure to **ask exactly what summer schools and exchange programmes are on offer** and how many students enrol in them.

**Ask about internships** and undergraduate research opportunities, both of which are valuable add-ons.

If you have strong preferences for a certain kind of assessment, **find out how students are evaluated** by looking at online course catalogues, module specifications and degree requirements. Using the same materials, you should be able to work out the kinds of modules within the programme that you'll have to take or you'll be able to choose. You can then hypothetically select a whole degree's worth of modules, required and optional, and judge for yourself whether studying them is a good way to spend three or four years of your life.

The college rankings compiled by *U.S. News & World Report* and the various league tables published in the UK are worth consulting, but they must be interpreted with some care. It's important to understand exactly what they're measuring. Some of the measurements have little to do with the quality of teaching that students receive. For example, some (but not all) of the universities that perform best on measurements of research excellence prioritize research and graduate training over undergraduate teaching, which is often farmed out to lower-paid adjuncts and postgraduate teaching assistants. The position of a particular university or programme may change dramatically in future rankings. One of the authors works at a university and supports a football team that are currently riding high in their respective league tables. This was not the case 10 years ago, and it would be surprising if it were still the case in 10 years' time. While there's no question that Russell Group universities and Ivy League schools have a valuable and stable reputation, other schools can possess different advantages, e.g. by offering more innovative programmes and more student focus as well as greater accessibility.

This chapter has argued that prospective students benefit from being aware of what data are available about the history programmes that interest them. Such information needs to be evaluated with care and doesn't necessarily make a difficult decision any easier. Understanding the basic purpose and career relevance of historical study and knowing how to navigate any programme to your best advantage are more important. Still, having a bit of a road map should be helpful both in making a choice and, later, in figuring out how to shape the best possible individual course of study in this field. Making the most of your time as a history undergraduate is the subject of the next chapter.

# CHAPTER 7

Learning history as an undergraduate

SO, WHAT'S IT LIKE TO study history at university? To say that everyone's experience is different might sound unhelpful, but it points to one feature that distinguishes university from school and history from many other degree subjects. At school, students generally study what their teachers put in front of them; teachers, in turn, teach what they're instructed to teach by examination boards or state-defined curricula. Universities enjoy much greater latitude. Accredited universities award their own qualifications and (at least in theory) respect the freedom of academics to speak their minds and share their expertise. This freedom is sometimes curtailed in practice by universities' desire to uphold their reputation in the eyes of students, parents, employers, competitors and both public and private funders. In more vocational subjects like engineering, what's taught is further restricted by professional organizations. Student choice in these subjects is correspondingly limited.

History possesses no equivalent professional accreditation schemes. UK history programmes are required to meet disciplinary 'benchmarks' set by a governmental body, and some US history programmes participate in a History Tuning Project coordinated by the AHA. On closer inspection, however, historians in both countries are purposely vague when describing the 'skills, knowledge and habits of mind' expected of a history graduate.[77] This vagueness doesn't stem from laxity or woolly-mindedness but from a recognition that there's a lot of history out there, and there are many ways to explore it. As a consequence, every history programme offers a different roster of modules, and every student will be given the opportunity to select from these modules to an extent unheard of in many other degrees.

History degrees, then, adhere to the notion that there are multiple paths to enlightenment, and that, by the same token, enlightenment is more a way of thinking than the absorption of a set body of knowledge. Indeed, one of the more disorienting aspects of studying history at university is that it makes us question why we think we know what we know, and why other historians might dispute our interpretations or the significance of our findings.

What makes history at university a form of 'higher education' is not that it teaches you about more and more places, periods and topics. Nor is it that university-educated historians necessarily attain greater certainty about the past. Knowing what you don't know or cannot know for sure is part of the historian's craft. The development of skills to find, evaluate and deploy information is an important element of any history degree, but, again, there's no quintessential historical method or methods that every undergraduate learns. History is a magpie discipline that borrows liberally from subjects as disparate as literary criticism and economics, with each historian developing their own toolkit of techniques. This doesn't flow from a rigid curriculum.

Ultimately, it's a 'higher education' because, whatever topics you study and whatever methods you learn, history degrees are designed to develop increasingly complex and sophisticated forms of thinking. Take a look at Figure 1: this shows Bloom's Taxonomy of Learning, which was devised by a group of American educational-ists in the mid-twentieth century to show how learning develops. At the bottom of the pyramid is 'Remember'. Yes, retaining information forms a large part of history at school, and it's a necessary foundation for more cerebral tasks – but it's only the first stage of the learning process. The second step, 'Understand', requires you to construct meaning out of the amassed information. Next comes the ability to 'Apply' this understanding to different settings. The top layers of the pyramid are more the province of learning at university than at school, and Chapter 2 suggested how historical thinking fits into these higher categories. Analysis involves comparing, contrasting and synthesizing different elements of information to ascertain how they relate to each other. Evaluation necessitates making your own judgements about the nature and significance of the information available. Creation is the pinnacle of learning, where your insight enables you to produce new meaning out of the information.

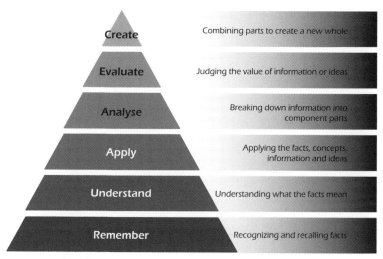

**Figure 1** Bloom's Taxonomy of Learning. Adapted from Jessica Shabatura's *Using Bloom's Taxonomy to Write Effective Learning Objectives*, 2018 (https://tips.uark.edu/using-blooms-taxonomy/).

This might sound rather abstract, and in practice it's not always possible to pinpoint what level of learning is being developed in a particular module or assignment. The general idea of a progression from lower-order to higher-order learning and thinking, however, is what gives undergraduate degrees their structure. In this chapter, we begin with the survey course, which often kicks things off in both the UK and the US. Then we consider the array of optional courses or modules, which is where American and British arrangements differ. Our third section focuses on the distinctive nature and impressive quality of history teaching. Finally, we turn to the importance of student initiative in crafting a successful university experience in historical study.

## Surveying surveys

Introductory modules at university concentrate on the fundamental tasks of remembering, understanding and applying information. This is the basis of survey modules, which are the mainstay of lower-level US history offerings and are a mandatory element of three-quarters of UK history programmes. Just as chemistry students would be lost without studying the periodic table, history students need to be acquainted with a narrative of significant events, people and trends, along with some preliminary work on higher analytical categories. Surveys aim to establish that bedrock of knowledge.

While this may seem straightforward enough, consider what those events, people and trends might be. A familiarity with Benedict Arnold and Harriet Tubman might seem indispensable to US students, but not to British ones. Conversely, the names Clement Attlee and Millicent Garrett Fawcett will probably mean nothing to US students. Meanwhile, students from both of these countries could graduate with flying colours without knowing a thing about the Canadian Confederation. And that's just to mention three modern Anglophone states. The past is vast, and even if you diligently learn to differentiate the Ming from the Qing dynasty, the Umayyad from the Abbasid caliphate and the Toltec from the Aztec empire, great expanses of time and space will remain entirely unknown to you. More pertinently, simply being able to associate a name with a period and a place is a feat of memory that represents no guarantee of understanding and still less of the higher-order forms of learning outlined by Bloom and his colleagues.

Comprehensiveness becomes even more fruitless an ambition when we consider that the past is expanding at a bewildering pace. This isn't due to the march of time – today becoming yesterday tomorrow – so much as the ever greater areas of human experience now being accepted as significant and knowable fields of historical inquiry (as we have seen in Chapter 5). Every past human activity, thought and experience is a legitimate subject for investigation, provided that evidence of it has survived. The histories of computer games, fear, baking, pet spiders, sexual harassment and pirates on film are all perfectly legitimate topics if researched in a methodical fashion. What's more, access to evidence has never been easier. Searchable digitized archives mean that needles can almost instantaneously be found in haystacks by historians who know what they're looking for. Current history surveys explicitly grapple with the need to acknowledge emerging fields of study and to incorporate primary source analysis.

American universities vary regarding what kinds of survey requirement apply to their history majors: sometimes it'll be on US history, sometimes Western or world history, and sometimes a combination. Regardless, it'll usually be part of the larger general education module. This variety is enhanced by different chronologies. One world history survey may begin in 1500, while another will reach back to the river valley civilizations. There's an assortment of periodizations in the US survey as well. The fact that survey courses may overlap with the types of history studied in high school is often acknowledged by excusing students with good Advanced Placement results from this particular exercise. However, for many students, surveys represent the entry point into their university programme.

UK universities offer no credit for pre-university courses. Instead, most require students to take surveys as preparation for higher-level study. A comparison of university survey courses and the subjects taught to British GCSE and A Level students indicates there's considerable overlap between the periods and places studied in the last years of school and the first years of university.

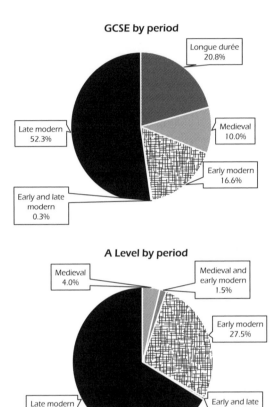

**GCSE by period**

Longue durée
20.8%

Medieval
10.0%

Early modern
16.6%

Early and late
modern
0.3%

Late modern
52.3%

**A Level by period**

Medieval
4.0%

Medieval and
early modern
1.5%

Early modern
27.5%

Early and late
modern
0.5%

Late modern
66.5%

**Figure 2** Chronological coverage of papers taken at GCSE and A Level for AQA, Edexcel and OCR qualifications, 2017–18. *Source:* AQA, Edexcel and OCR.

The statistics in Figures 2 and 3 have been kindly supplied by the three school examination boards who set the majority of GCSE and A Level exams (AQA, Edexcel and OCR); they thus exclude Scotland, which has its own education system with its own examinations. These figures allow us to see the periods and places studied by most history students in Britain during their last four years at school in order to compare them with the periods and places studied at university using the same research detailed in Chapter 6. The categories for period are ancient (before 500 CE), medieval (roughly 500–1500 CE), early modern (1500–1800 CE) and late modern (1800 CE to the present). Some of the exam topics spanned more than one of these periods, and a few encompassed all of them (what historians call the *longue durée*). The categories for place are self-explanatory.

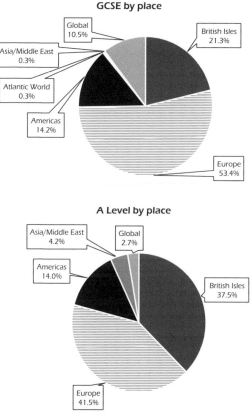

**Figure 3** Geographical coverage of papers taken at GCSE and A Level for AQA, Edexcel and OCR qualifications, 2017–18. *Source:* AQA, Edexcel and OCR.

The dominance of the late modern period and Europe at both A Level and GCSE is startling. These converge in the topics of Weimar and Nazi Germany and Tsarist and Communist Russia, which are extraordinarily if macabrely popular subjects among students (who are apparently obsessed with dictatorships). The second most popular A Level topics, early modern and British history, overlap in the topic of Tudor England. The standard combination at A Level of 'Hitler and the Henries' has been encouraged by requirements instituted by the erstwhile Secretary of State for Education Michael Gove in a cack-handed attempt to achieve the exact opposite. GCSE students are required to study one theme of British history over several centuries, which explains why 21% of papers concern the *longue durée*. Tudor England is once again very popular among GCSE students. US history is another much-studied topic, accounting for 14% of papers in both GCSE and A Level courses. Global history and non-Western history constitute just 7% of A Level and 11% of GCSE papers. Asia and the Middle East are seldom studied outside a global or imperial context. Africa and South America are entirely absent from the curriculum except when studied in broader topics in relation to empire, the slave trade, exploration or international relations.

Once a history student reaches university, they'll find that modules are as heavily slanted towards the late modern period as they were at school. Most UK university history degrees omit ancient history on the debatable grounds that it's a subject best left to those studying classics. Universities teach more mandatory medieval history separately or as part of longer time frames than is the case at A Level. A greater proportion of exclusively early modern courses are taken by sixth-formers or even GCSE students than are required to be taken by undergraduates. At half of the UK's universities, students aren't required to study a single module that focuses exclusively on the period before 1800.

Compulsory history modules at UK universities aren't quite as Eurocentric as most school history, although Britain and mainland Europe continue to command the most attention. More than half of UK history degrees include compulsory European modules, which account for the largest chunk (35%) of place-specific modules. Nearly half of history degrees require students to study modules dedicated to British history. The world beyond Britain and Europe is mostly covered in core modules on global history, which are mandatory at 50% of universities. A quarter of history degrees have core modules on either the Americas (generally North America) or the Atlantic World. In 2016, only two British universities required history students to study Asia-only modules, and none featured core modules that focused exclusively on Africa, South America or Oceania.

The considerable overlap between what British students study in school and what they study in compulsory survey modules at university can be viewed in different ways. From one perspective, it demonstrates a narrowness of vision, selecting from the vast range of possible historical subjects only those close to us in time and space. A more positive interpretation is that it eases students' passage into higher education by elaborating on familiar themes rather than ignoring everything they've learned in school. The same tension applies to the US as well, where introductory courses often cover topics already taken up in school surveys. In both the UK and the US, degrees are designed to facilitate a progression up Bloom's pyramid as well as the transition from school to university. History students are expected to move 'from breadth to depth, from tutelage to independence, from compulsion to choice and from critiquing to creating original historical research'.[78]

In reality, surveys constitute a minority of the required modules in the UK and only a small part of the history major in the US (typically around three to six credits of the 30-plus credits required in more advanced courses). Most core modules in both countries deal with the skills, methods and approaches used to study the past. These issues feature much less in history at school, which is more concerned with what happened and why as opposed to the knotty question of *how* we can establish what happened from our present-day vantage point. Dissertations are compulsory in four-fifths of UK history degrees. These are different from the personal projects that form part of some A Level assessments in that they're much larger undertakings and based on new research on primary sources rather than assessing other historians' work.

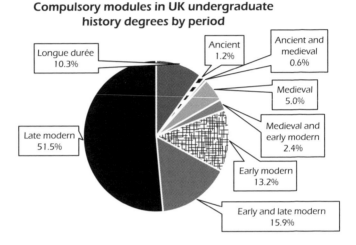

**Compulsory modules in UK undergraduate history degrees by period**

Longue durée 10.3%

Ancient 1.2%

Ancient and medieval 0.6%

Medieval 5.0%

Late modern 51.5%

Medieval and early modern 2.4%

Early modern 13.2%

Early and late modern 15.9%

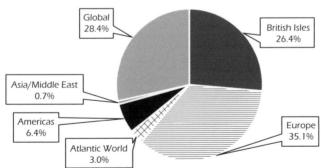

**Compulsory modules in UK undergraduate history degrees by place**

Global 28.4%

British Isles 26.4%

Asia/Middle East 0.7%

Americas 6.4%

Atlantic World 3.0%

Europe 35.1%

**Figure 4** Chronological and geographical coverage of compulsory modules in single-honours history degrees in the UK according to published programme specifications, 2016.

Requirements are broadly similar in US programmes after the introductory level, although there's considerable variation in the specifics. Most US history majors are required to take one or two courses on research methods, with the second involving an independent research project. While larger dissertations aren't usually compulsory unless you're an Honors student, they're available as options. Analysis, evaluation and creation – the highest forms of learning on Bloom's pyramid – are achieved when conducting original research, or at least that's the aim.

## Choosing options

The previous section made it clear that history students will need to fulfil some course requirements, but that's not to say they won't also enjoy a range of choices beyond these components – although patterns differ somewhat in the US and the UK.

In the former, history majors usually take at least eight courses of their own choosing (above the survey level). As noted in Chapter 4, there are usually a few stipulations to ensure that students aren't only covering modern (or premodern) or American history with their course selection. Increasingly, some programmes are also organizing sequences of three or four courses that will help students develop particular expertise in domains such as public history or digital history – but students can still decide whether or not to follow this route. Courses can be chosen to reflect particular interests in a region or subject matter, or even the reputation of the instructor(s) involved. You should also see this as an opportunity to experiment with a combination of more standard topics, such as political history, and some of the newer explorations of the past.

In most UK degree programmes, you'll choose more modules than you're assigned, with the breadth of choice increasing from one year to the next. Some universities take this to the extreme by asking you to create your own degree, selecting from a range of options at every stage (in essence, mirroring the US system). The opposite approach is taken by a dozen highly structured history programmes at New universities, where almost all of the modules are prescribed. Table 9 shows how options broaden your horizons not simply by providing you with more of a choice but also by introducing different ways to study the past. The proportion of case studies dealing with periods of under 30 years (roughly equivalent to A Level 'depth' studies) is six times higher in optional modules than in core ones. The former are also three times more likely than the latter to take a thematic approach by studying a topic in various historical contexts. For example, a colleague of ours teaches a module on slavery in global history, which compares the meaning, function and experience of slavery in the ancient world, the transatlantic slave trade and present-day human trafficking. Having a greater proportion of optional modules dealing with a specific theme and/or a relatively short period of time is generally a sign that these modules correspond to the teachers' research interests. By the same token, these modules will enable you to choose your own path, develop your own expertise and conduct your own research, helping you to become more skilled, specialized and independent by the time you graduate.

**Table 9** Type of compulsory and optional modules in UK history degree programmes according to published programme specifications, 2016.

|  | % of compulsory modules | % of optional modules |
| --- | --- | --- |
| Case study | 3.1 | 19.1 |
| Survey | 36.2 | 35.6 |
| Thematic | 11.2 | 36.3 |
| Skills, experience or research | 49.5 | 9.0 |

## How students experience studying history

History programmes aren't just collections of module requirements and options; they also involve different kinds of learning opportunities, such as working with faculty and pursuing special interests. History fares very well according to these vital, if somewhat more subjective, criteria: an important consideration when deciding whether or not to study the subject at university.

Most students enjoy their history programmes at least as much as their counterparts in other fields, and history instructors generally receive relatively high rankings for both their effectiveness and their concern for student success. It's not easy to measure teaching quality, but the subject is vital when considering how and what students actually learn.

The best available evidence about how students experience history degrees comes from the UK. Although there are no directly equivalent data for North America, the distinctive aspects of history teaching are evident on both sides of the Atlantic. So, with due allowance being made for the differences between nations and between institutions, the following surveys give a good idea of the pros (and occasional cons) of studying history at university. The British experience almost certainly holds true for students in the US as well.

The UK produces two annual surveys of undergraduates: the National Student Survey (NSS) and the Student Academic Experience Survey (SAES). The NSS is familiar to every British university student, each of whom is invited in their final year of study to answer 27 questions about the teaching, feedback, resources and engagement levels on their course. It is likewise well-known among prospective students and their parents because the resulting scores form a major component of the various league tables that rank each subject in each university. NSS results also feed into the Teaching

Excellence Framework: the government's means of rating teaching quality in higher education.

History's performance in the NSS is generally impressive compared with that of the 21 other subject groups taught to British undergraduates (see Table 11 in the appendix). In the most recent survey, history came fourth in terms of overall satisfaction, with 88% of students saying they were happy with the quality of their course. While history instructors were seemingly no better than average at responding to student views (Questions 23, 24 and 25), they received excellent marks for teaching ability (Questions 1 and 2), support (Questions 4 and 13) and most measures of feedback (Questions 9, 10 and 11). History was near the bottom of the pile with regard to offering opportunities for collaborative learning (Questions 21 and 22), and it underperformed relative to other subjects in terms of providing resources (Questions 18, 19 and 20). However, it outperformed most other subjects in the categories of student satisfaction with course content (Questions 3 and 5) and organization (Questions 15 and 16).

For a more reliable and detailed insight into what it's like to study history at university, it's necessary to turn to the SAES. This is because, unlike the NSS, the SAES surveys a representative sample of students. Every final-year student can take part in the NSS, but none is required to do so. This makes the NSS more akin to an election than a survey, with some students voting for their course and university, others voting against it and still others declining to participate at all. Another difference is that NSS results feed into league tables and other rankings, while SAES results do not. As a consequence, universities make considerable efforts to achieve positive NSS scores but have no incentive to do the same with regard to the SAES because its results aren't published on an institution-by-institution basis.

History students constitute only a few hundred of the roughly 14,000 students surveyed by the SAES each year. However, as the survey has been running in its current form since 2014, we can aggregate six years' worth of answers from a total of 2517 history students. As with the NSS, for each question the scores from history students have been ranked against those of students studying 20 other subjects, covering the whole gamut of undergraduate education from law to veterinary science.

History's performance in the SAES relative to other subjects (summarized in Table 12 in the appendix) shows that it's a distinctive and remarkably well-regarded subject to study in almost every respect. Its scores for teaching quality (Q4d.1 in Table 12) alone provide a compelling answer to the question 'Why study history?'. It was ranked the best subject to instigate debates and support independent learning, which, as we've said, are two of the core strengths of the history degree. This ability to investigate and discuss is vital not only in historical research but also in virtually any job.

The history degree was ranked second to creative arts and design degrees in motivating students and allowing them to pursue their own intellectual passions. History again placed second when it came to delivering structured sessions that engaged students' attention and explained concepts clearly, behind either linguistics and classics or its close cousins archaeology, philosophy and theology. The lowest-rated subject groups for these measures were in the STEM and business fields, where twice as many students found that their instructors struggled to explain concepts. Less than half of the students studying the same subjects thought that most or all of their teachers strove to make their subject interesting: a far cry from the three-quarters of history students who felt this way.

According to the SAES, history instructors matched or exceeded students' expectations of them (Q12d.1 and Q12d.2). The history students surveyed placed unusual emphasis on being taught by active researchers. What they encountered were teachers who appeared to be more research-active than anyone except those in the physical and biological sciences. History teachers were also considered to be exceptionally up to date on developments in the field and dedicated to improving their teaching.

The quality of feedback was another area in which history excelled (Q10c.1). History instructors were judged to be the most consistent at providing useful and timely feedback, at putting time and effort into their comments and at fielding follow-up questions. Only students of architecture, creative arts and design were more likely to receive face-to-face feedback and advice on drafts or their overall progress (Q10b). A quarter of engineering students reported that they normally received no comments on their assignments: just a grade. Only 3.5% of history students received the same perfunctory treatment. Twice as many history students as students of engineering, mathematics, business and administration, and medicine and dentistry credited their teachers with devoting considerable time to feedback.

Given the exceptional scores they gave to their instructors' methods, abilities and dedication, it's no surprise that history students were also the most likely to say their academic experience had surpassed their expectations (Q12). The subject areas of mass communications and technology performed worst on this question. It's also notable that 70% of history students said they'd learned a lot at university (Q12e). This score was bettered only by some content-heavy science degrees.

In 2017/18, when students were asked to provide an overall satisfaction rating, historical and philosophical studies (H&PS) came in joint-second place. A total of 88% of H&PS students were pleased with their education, which puts this subject group just behind the physical sciences and well ahead of the social sciences (80%) and arts and humanities as a whole (84%).

The SAES shines a light on differences in teaching methods as well as teaching quality. As we have seen, history placed the most emphasis on students debating each other in class. Discussion and debate were central to the majority of classes for 65% of history students. This is over three times the figure given by students in most STEM and business subjects. On top of this, history students were more likely to be encouraged to be self-reliant, to pursue their own interests and to conduct independent research. In these respects, history has more in common with project-based subjects such as architecture, creative arts and design than with other humanities subjects such as foreign languages.

History's emphasis on discussion and independent research means that its students' timetables often look very different from those of students taking other subjects. They reported receiving the smallest number of scheduled teaching sessions: a median figure of eight hours per week. This was two-thirds that of an average undergraduate and two-fifths that of a medical student. The smaller number of timetabled sessions for history students was matched by smaller class sizes. Half of their classes were seminars consisting of between one and fifteen students. History students spent a lot of time conducting independent research, meaning that their total hours of study were similar to those undertaking most other degrees.

The greater autonomy granted to history students has its advantages and its disadvantages, according to the survey. No other group of students felt they'd benefited more from independent study or had received as much help and support to point them in the right direction (Q5a.1 and Q4d.1). Yet the same methods that placed history at the top of some SAES rankings consigned it to the bottom of others, with history students the least satisfied with the amount of teaching they received. That they wanted more classroom time could be regarded as a backhanded compliment of sorts, especially given the high scores they awarded to their teachers. However, it explains the otherwise-incongruous statistic that history came sixteenth in the ranking of subjects deemed good or very good value for money (Q16).

When asked in a follow-up question how they were assessing value for money, dissatisfied students were twice as likely to mention high tuition fees and low contact hours as any other factor. They had relatively few complaints about what they studied or how it was taught, and – contrary to the popular assumption that history offers poor career prospects – they weren't particularly concerned about 'the likelihood of getting a well-paid job on graduation.' Students who considered history degrees to be good or very good value cited excellent teaching, subject matter and resources as the main reasons for their satisfaction. Studying history therefore appears to involve a trade-off between the quality and quantity of teaching. While history students appreciated learning from talented and committed teachers who offered stimulating lessons and provided tailor-made feedback and support, some were left wanting more.

As noted, the US doesn't generate the kind of cumulative data about teaching that's available in the UK. But almost every university regularly surveys students about the quality of instruction in each course, and the results are accumulated across disciplines annually. In these evaluations, history instructors and courses do remarkably well when compared with those of other disciplines.

Overall, teaching surveys on both sides of the Atlantic point to characteristics of history degrees that will suit some temperaments more than others. History is an ideal degree for intellectually curious, self-motivated people who like to find out things for themselves and stake out positions. As a general rule, history students aren't pack animals, although many programmes are introducing greater opportunities for group work. They're active learners who reach their own judgements about ambiguous evidence and complex, often conflicting explanations. Their instructors model the qualities demonstrated by successful history students: passion, dedication, organization, communication, responsibility and consideration towards others.

If you don't like analysing, debating and presenting findings after independent research, then studying history possibly isn't for you. If you do, then you have the skills not only to perform well in a history degree but also to prosper after graduation in the lion's share of professional and managerial careers.

## Taking charge of your history education

The quality of your education has less to do with what you study or where you study than *how* you study. That's the central message of some fascinating research that's been undertaken over the past five years in the US by Gallup, in collaboration with Purdue University and the Strada Education Network. After interviewing tens of thousands of alumni and current students, they identified six experiences at university that are strongly associated with three positive outcomes. These outcomes are

(1) considering a degree to have been value for money,

(2) being an 'engaged employee' after graduating,

(3) reporting high levels of well-being in other aspects of post-university life.

It's important to bear in mind that correlation isn't causation. It may be that the people who had a great time at college, enjoy their work and are happy with their day-to-day existence, social life, neighbourhood, finances and physical health aren't like you, or at least aren't like me. In other words, that they're the kind of (justifiably) smug individuals whose Facebook posts bear some resemblance to their everyday life. Even so, the six student experiences pinpointed by Gallup (Table 10) sound like the sorts of things that would benefit anyone.

It's therefore disconcerting that only one of the six statements elicited strong agreement from the majority of current students or alumni: 'I had at least one professor at [college] who made me excited about learning.' So, most students encountered at least one inspirational instructor, but just a quarter or so strongly agreed that teachers cared for them or mentored them or worked with them on a lengthy project. The proportion who gained relevant work experience or threw themselves into extracurricular activities was also very much in the minority. Altogether, a mere 3% of alumni ticked each of the six boxes with alacrity and without hesitation.[79]

**Table 10** Valued experiences of college and university reported by alumni and currently enrolled undergraduates, 2014 and 2017. Gallup 2014/2017. Data from Gallup and Purdue University, *Great Jobs, Great Lives*, p. 9; Steve Crabtree, 2019, 'Six college experiences linked to student confidence on jobs', *Gallup News*, January 22 (https://bit.ly/3bNNnCp).

| | % of alumni | % of current undergraduates |
|---|---|---|
| I had at least one professor at [college] who made me excited about learning | 63 | 57 |
| My professors at [college] cared about me as a person | 27 | 27 |
| I had a mentor who encouraged me to pursue my goals and dreams | 22 | 25 |
| I worked on a project that took a semester or more to complete | 32 | 24 |
| I had an internship or job that allowed me to apply what I was learning in the classroom | 29 | 40 |
| I was extremely active in extracurricular activities and organizations | 20 | 18 |

It should be noted that these data derive from undergraduate programmes in general, not just history. However, they do offer some potential guidance to history students and the faculty who work with them. To wit, how do you go about becoming one of the select 3% of fully realized students, or at least how do you graduate without too many regrets over opportunities missed and skills unlearned? Gallup offers the following advice:

► As best you can, pick professors, not courses. Seek professors who have reputations for being amazing teachers and mentors.

► Invest in a mentor. This goes both ways – [choose] someone who agrees to or offers to mentor you as well as someone you feel is worth the investment of your time.

► Find a job or internship where you can apply what you're learning, or work to connect what you're learning to your current job.

► Take at least a couple of courses that involve long-term projects requiring a semester or more of work to complete.

► Don't try to 'pad your résumé' with a long list of extracurricular activities; get deeply, lastingly engaged in at least one.[80]

Fortunately, the way history is taught at university provides exceptional possibilities to achieve all but one of these experiences.

The best way of developing meaningful relationships with your teachers is to get to know them in seminars or other small classes. You might be little more than a face in the crowd of a packed lecture hall at first, but this will end once you start discussing ideas with your instructors in a small-group setting and they begin reading your work. Small-group teaching is a hallmark of upper-level courses in the humanities.

Perhaps because of the smaller class sizes, or perhaps because humanities faculty simply exude humanity, Gallup found that 43% of the professors who had mentored recent graduates taught in the arts and humanities. This was five times the number of mentors who taught business and twice the number who taught social sciences.[81] Among students still at university, those in the arts and humanities were more likely than others to have encountered inspiring lecturers who cared about them and supported their aspirations.[82]

History students' ability to undertake extracurricular activities is a compensation of sorts for their lower levels of time in the classroom. As we discovered earlier, history students in the UK spend an average of eight hours per week in class and another 18 hours on independent study, fieldwork or placements. When you take these 26 hours of studying per week out of the equation (and allow for the leisurely mornings beloved by so many undergraduates), this leaves history students several hours a day to volunteer, play sport, join societies, do paid work and generally beef up their résumés. It's fundamentally a matter of motivation.

Finding the right internship is the one experience in which history students have no obvious advantage. As we have seen in Chapter 2, history graduates end up in an extraordinary range of occupations, which means it can be hard as a student to know where to start. The important thing to keep in mind is that a history degree disqualifies you from very few careers. If you want to become a history teacher, researcher or museum curator, great. However, more of the history students we work with are interested in fields such as human resources, marketing or law. They discover that these sectors are as open to history interns as to anyone else. To give you a sense of the possibilities, here's a list of the placements obtained last year by students we're currently teaching:

- three worked at IBM;
- two worked at the Confederation of British Industry;
- two worked for marketing agencies;
- two worked for recruitment agencies;
- two taught English abroad;
- one did publicity work for a university; and
- the rest landed graduate-level placements at multinationals including the manufacturer Unilever, the accounting firm Ernst & Young, the supermarket Aldi, the sports retailer Decathalon and Enterprise Rent-A-Car.

As you can see, none undertook a placement directly related to history. The advantages of obtaining relevant work experience before graduation are obvious enough. According to the most recent survey by the National Association of Colleges and Employers in the US, over half of internships resulted in the offer of a permanent job.[83]

This and other chapters have shown that history students have many opportunities, but also important responsibilities, to take an active role in planning their university programme. Once they've fulfilled their requirements, they've got lots of latitude in selecting courses, modules and instructors. They can develop skills through extracurricular activities and internships as well as via independent research projects as part of their degree. They're extremely likely to work with teachers of high quality and to be pleased with their programme of study. They'll also have an unusual degree of freedom to pursue particular intellectual interests and to discover new ones during their time at university.

Studying history will equip you with a variety of skills relevant to obtaining a wide range of rewarding jobs. The discipline features above-average teachers and learning experiences alongside opportunities to gain additional strengths through intelligent planning and initiative. History also prepares students, no matter their career path, for responsible citizenship, engendering public service and personal satisfaction. This will be the focus of our next chapter.

# PART IV

## HISTORY AS A PUBLIC GOOD

# CHAPTER 8

In public service: why society needs history
and historians

SO FAR, THIS BOOK HAS emphasized three basic topics: first, a discussion of what history learning is and how it has been changing; second, how studying history prepares people for rewarding careers; and third, what students can do to maximize their opportunities in history programmes. This chapter offers a somewhat different final argument, although it's closely related to our point about historical skills. Trained historians and informed history graduates are vital to a healthy democratic society, and this is another reason to engage in the discipline besides career training and basic human curiosity. At this moment in time, when democratic societies are being challenged, historical analysis provides an essential service.

This argument – that historical study has a crucial social function – is complicated in at least two ways. First, we live in an age of partisanship, which is inevitably spilling over into debates about history. Some people, even in the US and the UK, are no longer convinced that a liberal democracy is worth much and so may dismiss the arguments of this chapter. Second, and even more troubling, we know for a fact that many citizens leave school with a startling lack of basic historical knowledge. We also know that this isn't a new problem. The historian and educationalist Sam Wineburg has studied test results at various points from the early twentieth century onwards that show Americans have often been shockingly unaware of basic facts about the past.[84]

Arguably, these problems can be turned on their heads. The social contribution made by historical thinking increases in periods of political polarization. Moreover, the tenuous grasp of history possessed by many people makes it all the more important for professionally trained historians to share their knowledge. Even Wineburg, who is critical of many past efforts at teaching history, points to better opportunities in the future.

This chapter lays out several ways in which historical thinking and research serve as contributions to society, not instead of their role in career preparation but alongside it. The discipline's social value is based in part on its key skills, including the ability to spot fake news (and fake claims of fake news). History builds on what we know about assessing analogies, which crop up so often in public life, and the cultural construction of identity.

Many people – not just historians! – speak passionately about the importance of historical perspective or the ability to use historical reference points when dealing with contemporary issues. These claims are valid and important, but this chapter will try to be more specific, using what we know about historical thinking and defining the applications of perspective in greater detail. Our discussion of history's topical range (see Chapter 5) provides an important basis for its further applications: historical inquiry and knowledge can apply not only to politics, diplomacy and war – those vital but familiar avenues – but also to considerations of environmental issues, relationships between culture change and economic factors, patterns of crime and policing, and the framework of family life. Historians are ready and able to contribute a deep understanding of patterns of change and continuity to a variety of subject areas.

Our societies today, and their position in the wider world, have been shaped and continue to be shaped by developments in the past. While we work to promote desirable historical understanding in schools, we also need people in a plethora of careers who have pursued the connections between the present and the past in greater depth, both at university level and beyond.

## Striving for accuracy

One of the first things a new authoritarian regime will do is rewrite school history books. Cooking up a supportive story that bolsters the current ruling group and vilifies any opposition is an essential part of suppressing dissent. In Nazi Germany, changes were made to the school curriculum to portray the rise and superiority of the Aryan race. In East Germany, students were taught that communists, not Jews, were the primary victims of Hitler's tyranny. Students in the Soviet Union studied protests in US history as case studies of the collapse of capitalism. And so on.[85]

Our first claim about history's service to society, then, is that it's really important to have historians to provide us with a balanced and accurate treatment of the past – which, as we've just seen, is open to discussion and revision. This call for a commitment to accuracy is not just an indictment of authoritarian regimes, past or present; it applies to the here and now. In 2010, the *Washington Post* outed a textbook that was required reading for fourth-graders in Virginia's public schools. The book claimed that 'thousands of Southern blacks fought in Confederate ranks', implying that many African Americans spontaneously sided with the Confederacy regardless of slavery.[86] This is simply false, as historians were quick to demonstrate – and not only false, but part of a long-standing effort to downplay the impact of slavery in Southern life in ways that have grossly distorted the historical experience of African Americans. The concern for historical truth should start at home.

## Learning from the past

The classic point has already been made, but it applies whole-heartedly to the social uses of historical study: if we don't attend to history, we are liable to repeat past errors and injustices. It's easiest to see the need for historical correction when it applies to other people. After World War II, the Allies insisted that Germany and Japan be taught the errors of their past as a means of nurturing democratic and anti-militaristic values. These efforts broadly worked, although concerns persist that Japan has not fully confronted its war crimes, and a minority of right-wing Germans currently seem intent on forgetting their nation's history.[87] A willingness to ponder past mistakes has nonetheless been integral to the post-war cultural transformation of both countries.

The same process of historical reflection has taken place in English-speaking countries. Americans have come to recognize that the internment of Japanese Americans in World War II was a policy that should never be repeated. After 9/11, President George W. Bush was very careful to reject any such plans for Muslim Americans. In recent decades, Australians and Canadians have used historical study to inform a revised view of their treatment of aboriginal populations, leading not only to public apologies but also to substantive policy changes. It's admittedly difficult to confront past wrongs or even engage in unpleasant discussions. As we noted in Chapter 5, protests from veterans and nationalist groups in 1995 forced the Smithsonian to water down a presentation that questioned the necessity of dropping atomic bombs on Japan 50 years earlier. At the time of writing, while most Americans admit the 2003 invasion of Iraq was a mistake, it's not yet possible to explore this issue extensively in public school history because of current nationalist passions. Looking objectively at recent history can be particularly challenging.

If history warns us against repeating past errors, it also provides examples of constructive policies that should be remembered today. Recently, a group of economists have been discussing the desirability of a new field they call Progress Science. Under this mantle, they propose to take past cases of what they view as successful activities to see if they can draw out any ingredients that might be useful now. For example, why did Silicon Valley instead of, say, Chicago or Atlanta end up being the heart of the US's high-tech industry; and why did the Industrial Revolution occur when it did?[88]

Historians might quiver a bit at this approach. They, of all people, are aware of the difficulty of teasing out causal factors, and some would dispute the characterization of industrialization as a straightforward success story. It's nonetheless possible to argue that historians have spent too much time seeing history as a warning against error and not enough time mining it for information to guide positive action. It was recently suggested by a historian that anyone contemplating the possibility of peace in the Middle East should know something about the Treaty of Westphalia of 1648, which succeeded in reducing religious strife in Europe.[89] In the US, another historian encouraged her readers to look at the successful aspects of federal housing policy a few decades ago and urged that some elements be recaptured now.[90]

No historian would claim that we can dissect a past situation and use it as a blueprint for making a major decision today. But organizations such as History and Policy in the UK and websites such as Allen Mikaelian's *Checkered History* project in the US show how the past – if treated carefully – can profitably inform present-day policymaking and debate.[91]

Finally, beyond warnings about past mistakes and injustices, contributing positive lessons and evaluating analogies, it's crucial to remember that our present is directly shaped by trends that emerge from the past. One of the reasons that so many criminologists now routinely turn to history is because current crime patterns are the result of decades-long evolution. Discussions about the falling birth rate in many societies today and its possibly troubling implications for the future are the result of tracing trajectories back over more than a century. Knowing how to obtain historical data on developments of this sort and understanding how to evaluate and contextualize that data are basic components of good policy. Here, too, historical training is essential.

*Applying history to the Covid-19 crisis of 2020*

Epidemics are not new, and there's a rich history to orient us in current challenges. Indeed, the history of epidemics is one of those fields that historians have explored in depth as part of their expanded research agenda.[92] At the same time, epidemiologists themselves use history as an integral part of their own calculations about how disease spreads and how societies respond. Recent examples, such as the dreadful 'Spanish' flu of 1918–19 or the 'Asian' flu of 1957, are particularly salient, but earlier cases can help to inform us as well.

There are several basic points we can make here. First, devastating plagues used to be far more common than they are today: in Europe, for example, they occurred about every 20–30 years in the seventeenth century, and then again in the early nineteenth century, when cholera was the main scourge. Amsterdam had at least three outbreaks of bubonic plague in the seventeenth century, each killing about 10% of the population. Yet societies can bounce back: plagues often bring out shining examples of generosity and empathy. However, thinking about past epidemics also reminds us of widespread fear; of minority groups being attacked or foreigners being blamed for an outbreak; of widening gaps between the rich, who could afford to escape, and the poor, who bore the brunt; and of authorities trying to lie about the depth of the problem in an attempt to avoid criticism. These are features which also surfaced in 2020 that we need to minimize, using past problems as a guide.

Epidemiologists can point to more specific connections between past and present. Modern pandemics – a term that was invented in 1853 – spread very rapidly, as Covid-19 has done. Furthermore, they often come in waves: the Spanish flu, for instance, came in two, and the second, striking young people disproportionately, was far worse than the first. The crisis of spring 2020 is almost certainly the first of several we need to prepare for.

Finally, historical analysis highlights what's new about the Covid-19 dilemma, including the amusing fact that concerns about toilet paper shortages are a novel component of epidemic response: the fruit of changing hygiene. We came to this crisis with unprecedented organizational capacity (as several Asian societies demonstrated), but also with unprecedented expectations, even compared with just a century ago. We're less tolerant of death now: the Spanish flu created huge dislocations, but it wasn't seen as totally surprising, which may have speeded recovery. The 2020 crisis is more profound: we're more reliant on hospitals, but less willing to try to care for acutely ill people at home. These new standards are deeply ingrained. They're admirable in many ways, but they've made the task of responding to the crisis unusually difficult. Here, too, history provides vital ways for us to calibrate our response.

## Seeking greater agreement

Recently, an intriguing argument has resurfaced about the importance a national historical narrative might have in helping to correct the fractured society around us. This argument has some shortcomings, and it places some contemporary historians in a not entirely favourable light; but it's worth discussing as another facet of the public service history offers. In the US, historian Jill Lepore contends that one of the reasons for the intensity of the partisan divide in current political life is the decline of an agreed-upon national story being taught in schools and carried forward into public culture.[93] There's something of a chicken-and-egg situation here. Crafting an accepted national story becomes more difficult when liberals and conservatives are shouting at each other. While it's tempting for historians to remain above the fray, the culture wars over issues such as whether Confederate monuments should be allowed to remain standing desperately need informed historical perspectives. By contributing their expertise to debates over the most contentious aspects of national pasts – for example, the legacy of racism in the US and imperialism in Britain – historians perform a major civic duty.

The changes we've seen in historical research over the past few decades mean that any plausible national narrative we came up with now would diverge significantly from the patriotic simplifications that were once the mainstay of history textbooks (and that still survive in some popular histories). The work of social historians means that discrimination against subordinate groups including the poor, the disabled, women, and sexual and ethnic minorities can no longer be consigned to the margins. Research by world historians has undercut national histories that are insular and self-regarding. These twin strands of combatting marginalization and comprehending globalization are coming together in Britain's current soul-searching about its imperial past. Drawing attention to the exploitative nature of imperialism as an integral element in British history is a vital corrective to unbridled nationalism. These efforts to 'decolonize the curriculum' constitute an example of how history can help frame (and be framed by) social and political imperatives. At the same time, the fact that we need to admit real complexity is not an argument against the importance of building a coherent national story.

## Nostalgia and optimism

Most people have some sense of how the past relates to the present. Correspondingly, another way that historians and history students provide a public service is by offering ways to enhance the understandings involved – not necessarily to shoot them down, but to encourage more thoughtful orientations. Some cultures have viewed the relationship between then and now in terms of cycles. More common still is the sense that some challenging current developments can be better understood via comparisons with similar patterns in the past, yielding our almost inevitable fascination with analogies. Here, as we've seen, historians have an active role to play in figuring out how analogies might be applied and how they need to be amended.

Nostalgia feeds another common use of history: insisting that, in some major way, the past was better than the present. It's incumbent on historians to tease out the implications of nostalgic arguments about when, for example, family life is thought to have been better than it is today: when children were more obedient, when divorce rates were lower, when love was less complicated. Excessive nostalgia is often shoddy history, based on myths of a past golden age and used to justify a contemporary political or theological viewpoint.[94]

Conversely, a belief in progress may lead people to view the past and present alike as prefiguring an ever-improving future. Optimism itself has a history. The term was coined in eighteenth-century France, and today's optimists hark back to the age of Enlightenment to justify their own faith in a future of scientific rationality.[95] Again, historians can provide a note of caution here. Optimists' selective reading of the past for prefigurations of progress (what is termed 'Whiggery') is often as crude and simplistic an approach as excessive nostalgia, and their visions of the future tend to age poorly. Historical knowledge and thinking skills provide a necessary counterbalance to brash futurism.

Popular readings of the past may be invested with great passion. One of the most powerful motives for protest, for example, lies in a belief that present conditions are deteriorating (an argument that's currently being used to justify curbing immigration) or that long-standing injustices can no longer be allowed to continue (a sentiment captured by the Time's Up movement). Contemporary identities are often grounded in narratives of the past, which can stretch back a long way. The Yugoslav Wars between 1991 and 2001 were fuelled in part by rival interpretations of battles fought several centuries earlier. Korean attitudes towards Japan continue to be overshadowed by memories of the sexual abuse experienced by 'comfort women' during World War II. For many African Americans or native Americans, past persecutions aren't so much memories as active components of their current outlook. Historians needn't undercut passion, and indeed they may share it, but they should encourage careful assessment.

The point is, people have their own views of history whether or not they think of them as such. These views may be nostalgic, optimistic, impassioned or something else entirely, but they connect large publics to interpretations of the past. Current actions, at the political level and beyond, flow from these orientations. The historian's role is not that of infallible expert bent on exposing other people's exaggerations and emotions or rendering definitive judgements about What Really Happened. After all, academics make their living by disagreeing among themselves. Historians nonetheless have a social obligation to speak out against the distortion and misuse of history, and to identify and understand the models of history that shape personal identity and infuse public debate.

The connections between past and present are inescapable. One of the reasons studying history is so fascinating is that it impels us to engage with past patterns from which our present has emerged. This engagement is not only interesting but plays a crucial role in encouraging a more accurate and constructive grasp of the concerns of our own time, including issues of basic citizenship.

Take, for example, the contemporary discourse on voting rights in the US. Debate surges over how electoral districts are defined and how groups are encouraged or impeded in the voting process. A historical perspective is needed when considering these issues' roots in a Constitution written in the eighteenth century, the practices of gerrymandering and Jim Crow developed and named in the nineteenth century, and the civil rights struggles that led to the Voting

Rights Act of 1965. People who are legitimately concerned with the current problem of voting rights, in other words, should know something of the history of voting rights; it will provide them with greater understanding and better arguments. That same counsel applies to Brexit: in order to get your head around what's now taking shape, it's important to understand the evolution of British–European relations and how past tensions and collaborations may contribute to future possibilities.

History has been regarded as essential to citizenship for a variety of reasons, not all equally valid. Used to service overblown nationalism, it can distort and mislead, but, studied with care, it can provide the foundations of responsible democratic participation. In 2019, during an inquiry into the policies of President Donald Trump, a key witness was Fiona Hill, who was born in County Durham in the UK and initially trained in history and Russian at the University of St Andrews in Scotland. Now an American citizen, Harvard PhD and Russian policy expert, Hill offered a careful and measured assessment of recent developments. Her testimony ended with the statement:

> *I have no interest in advancing your inquiry in any particular direction, except towards the truth.*[96]

These words reflect real political courage on her part at a time of inflamed political passion. They also express the civic power – in this case, the transatlantic power – of robust historical training.

History doesn't answer all social questions. It provokes disagreement and argumentation. But, earnestly consulted and responsibly interpreted, history does help humanity in its never-ending quest for truth and understanding. History students actively participate in this quest at university and beyond, making their lives – and those of the people around them – more meaningful and useful in the process. Why study history? Because there's a true calling here.

*Further reading*

See 'History and citizenship' on the Historical Association's website (https://bit.ly/3bVXcyg). See also Laura Puaca's 2004 article 'History, democracy and citizenship: the debate over history's role in teaching citizenship and patriotism' on the website of the Organization of American Historians (https://bit.ly/2HGX9s5).

For a fascinating discussion on an effort to apply family history to policy, see John Demos's *Past, Present and Personal: The Family and the Life Course in American History* (New York: Oxford University Press, 1988).

# CONCLUSION

THIS BOOK HAS ARGUED, QUITE simply, that if you like studying history, at least a good bit of the time, then deciding to focus on history at university could be the right choice for you. Even if you don't like it too much, it might still be a good idea to get some university-level exposure to history (just as it can be useful for students who don't like mathematics to be prompted to do a bit more of it).

Happily, a good number of students *do* like to study history. This includes people who have grown to love the subject at school as well as students who find out at university that history has dimensions they hadn't appreciated before. We've seen how history's expanding subject matter and the positive response rates to history teachers at university provide additional reasons to consider historical study.

Probably the most consequential claims in this book, carefully supported by data, are that history graduates can expect good job outcomes and the related fact that most go on to fields other than teaching. (At the risk of having our cake and eating it, we also note that history teachers and public historians provide vital services and often report high job satisfaction.) Those who study history end up in all sorts of jobs, with average earnings that rival those of people in most other fields and, again, with comparatively strong reports of job satisfaction.

This book has also explained why history students fare so well in their careers, and this point deserves emphasis as well. The range of topics students explore and, above all, the skills they develop or enhance in their history courses go far beyond successfully memorizing all the Chinese dynasties or the definition of the Renaissance. Experience in evaluating data, building persuasive arguments, thinking critically, and assessing change and continuity: these are all abilities that can be carried forward easily.

These same abilities will have staying power even in a changing economy. Every forecast of the future job market emphasizes many of the capacities historical study helps to generate, including adaptability and dealing with ambiguity.

While it's true that history graduates often take a bit more time to settle into careers than those in some other fields, the fact that choosing to study history is not the same thing as identifying a single career path may be something of a plus. It offers you plenty of time for mature consideration, for one. Nevertheless, this pattern should be acknowledged.

Still, the positive data are truly reassuring, and they deserve to be emphasized in order to combat some of the more negative stereotypes about history as a subject. To repeat the point we made earlier: students choosing history, and the anxious parents of those students, can rest assured that a history focus is a solid career move.

Before they graduate into the job market, history students can add to their credentials through intentional efforts during their university careers. Such efforts include being aware of the kinds of habits of mind they're enhancing and developing the ability to discuss these with potential employers and others. They also include sampling different kinds of historical topics, curating a careful balance between more traditional and new approaches (including opportunities in public or digital history). Signing up for a deliberate admixture of work in other disciplines as well as taking advantage of at least some of the varied extracurricular activities available at university are also advisable. Finally, having early and regular interaction with careers services – an area where some history students currently seem to lag – is highly recommended.

History programmes are also increasingly emphasizing the availability of internships in a variety of fields as well as more independent research projects, both of which deliberately link history training with wider experience. Alert students can and should take advantage of these opportunities.

The point here is clear: the decision to study history is sensible for all sorts of reasons, but you must put careful thought into how to make the most of the opportunity.

This book has also emphasized the importance of history and historical skills in citizenship and public service, regardless of the career path you choose. These are challenging political times, on both sides of the Atlantic, and the need for people with real experience both in assessing data and arguments and in applying historical perspective to the issues of the day may truly be greater than at any other period in the recent past.

A final point. Way back in Chapter 1, we noted that there were three reasons to study history: it leads to good jobs, it's a great way to build skills and gain a better understanding of the human condition, and, quite simply, it's a pleasure. We emphasized that this book would be paying primary attention to the jobs and understanding arguments, which are closely related. However, we think it's time, in closing, to go back to joy – or at least, as Gilbert and Sullivan once said, modified rapture.

Studying history is not always fun (nor is studying anything): some topics may not appeal; the pressure of coursework and exams can be wearying; a few teachers may misfire. Yet learning about the past and how it connects to the present – whether directly or through analogy or example – can be truly engaging. The ability to go from 'I didn't know that had a history' or 'What's the history of that?' to a real interaction with past patterns and processes of change and continuity is thrilling!

A couple of years ago, one of the authors, while working with two students, finally had the chance to answer a question he'd been chewing over for some time: when and why did celebrating birthdays become common? The findings were arguably 'significant' in that the rise of the birthday signalled new beliefs about the nature of childhood and happiness. Beyond this, the process of thinking about the subject and uncovering new data (including some interesting though ultimately abortive resistance to the rise of the birthday) was simply entertaining: a joy of discovery that history frequently offers either through new research or by contemplating the innovative findings of other people. We believe the two students had the same experience; both, in fact, have gone on to research projects of their own, even though one of them had not planned to do so.

None of this detracts from the serious and practical reasons to study history. But it's worth emphasizing that, no matter which of the many, many career opportunities a history student ultimately selects, the opportunity for periodic engagement with the joy of discovery and with new stances on why people and societies behave as they do is always available – whether or not it's always career relevant. History is a truly utilitarian career choice; but it's more than that, and life should be, too.

The goals of this book will be amply met if students find it useful in figuring out why (or even why not) to study history; if it gives them a better grasp of how to plan their work in history for optimal career and personal benefit; and if it has opened their eyes to the fact that everything has a history – a realization that will result in wide-ranging opportunities for intellectual engagement, at university and beyond.

# APPENDIX

How students experience UK history degrees

**Table 11** Satisfaction scores and rankings for history in National Student Survey, 2019.

|  | Ranking of history (out of 22 subjects) | % history students agreeing |
|---|---|---|
| 1. Staff are good at explaining things | 2 | 93.5 |
| 2. Staff have made the subject interesting | 2 | 90.6 |
| 11. I have received helpful comments on my work | 2 | 83.0 |
| 5. My course has provided me with opportunities to explore ideas or concepts in depth | 3 | 88.6 |
| 16. The timetable works efficiently for me | 3 | 82.2 |
| 12. I have been able to contact staff when I needed to | 4 | 90.1 |
| 15. The course is well organized and running smoothly | 4 | 77.6 |
| 27. Overall, I am satisfied with the quality of the course | 4 | 88.1 |
| 9. Marking and assessment has been fair | 5 | 78.0 |
| 3. The course is intellectually stimulating | 6 | 90.8 |
| 13. I have received sufficient advice and guidance in relation to my course | 6 | 80.0 |
| 10. Feedback on my work has been timely | 8 | 76.5 |
| 19. The library resources (e.g. books, online services and learning spaces) have supported my learning well | 8 | 88.0 |
| 24. Staff value students' views and opinions about the course | 8 | 76.7 |
| 17. Any changes in the course or teaching have been communicated effectively | 9 | 79.6 |
| 23. I have had the right opportunities to provide feedback on my course | 10 | 85.0 |

| | Ranking of history (out of 22 subjects) | % history students agreeing |
|---|---|---|
| 4. My course has challenged me to achieve my best work | 12 | 81.3 |
| 8. The criteria used in marking have been clear in advance | 12 | 73.0 |
| 6. My course has provided me with opportunities to bring information and ideas together from different topics | 14 | 84.4 |
| 14. Good advice was available when I needed to make study choices on my course | 16 | 73.7 |
| 20. I have been able to access course-specific resources (e.g. equipment, facilities, software, collections) when I needed to | 18 | 85.3 |
| 22. I have had the right opportunities to work with other students as part of my course | 18 | 75.8 |
| 7. My course has provided me with opportunities to apply what I have learned | 19 | 76.2 |
| 18. The IT resources and facilities provided have supported my learning well | 20 | 80.7 |
| 21. I feel part of a community of staff and students | 20 | 61.3 |
| 25. It is clear how students' feedback on the course has been acted on | 21 | 51.8 |
| 26. The students' union (association or guild) effectively represents students' academic interests | 22 | 46.2 |

**Table 12** History compared with other subject groups in Student Academic Experience Survey, 2014–19. $N$ = 87,278, of whom 2,517 were history undergraduates.

| | Rank (out of 21 subjects) | % | |
| --- | --- | --- | --- |
| | | History students | All students |
| **Teaching** | | | |
| **Q4d.1. Thinking about all the teaching you have experienced this year, what proportion of teaching staff did the following? (answering all/majority)** | | | |
| Regularly initiated debates and discussions | 1 | 65.1 | 35.2 |
| Encouraged you to take responsibility for your own learning | 1 | 85.1 | 78.4 |
| Used lectures/teaching groups to guide and support independent study | 1 | 68.4 | 56.7 |
| Motivated you to do your best work | 2 | 61.8 | 51.7 |
| Helped you explore your own areas of interest | 2 | 45.8 | 32.8 |
| Worked hard to make their subjects interesting | 2 | 71.5 | 55.9 |
| Clearly explained course goals and requirements | 2 | 69.4 | 64.6 |
| Were helpful and supportive | 3 | 75.0 | 67.0 |
| Didn't make it clear what was expected of you | 18 | 10.6 | 13.2 |
| Were poor at explaining things | 20 | 4.1 | 8.3 |
| Taught in an unstructured and disorganized way | 20 | 5.4 | 8.7 |
| **Q5a.1. To what extent do you agree or disagree with the following statements? (agree/strongly agree)** | | | |
| I feel I have benefited from the independent study that I have done this year | 1 | 77.3 | 70.4 |

| | Rank (out of 21 subjects) | %  | |
|---|---|---|---|
| | | History students | All students |
| **Teaching (continued)** | | | |
| It is easy to schedule time to discuss work, or discuss work on email, outside of scheduled contact hours | 3 | 74.6 | 64.5 |
| I feel I have sufficient access to academic staff outside timetabled sessions in order to discuss aspects of my work (this includes email as well as face-to-face) | 4 | 75.3 | 68.4 |

### Q12d.1. How important to you are the following characteristics of teaching staff? (very important)

| | Rank | History | All |
|---|---|---|---|
| They are currently active researchers in their subject | 2 | 33.2 | 24.2 |
| They maintain and improve their subject knowledge on a regular basis | 11= | 58.8 | 58.0 |
| They have received training in how to teach | 16 | 57.5 | 60.2 |
| They have relevant industry or professional expertise | 16 | 36.1 | 45.4 |
| They employ original/creative teaching methods | 19 | 31.0 | 35.3 |
| They maintain and improve their teaching skills on a regular basis | 20 | 45.6 | 51.2 |

### Q12d.2. To what extent do you feel your teaching staff currently demonstrate these characteristics? (very much)

| | Rank | History | All |
|---|---|---|---|
| They are currently active researchers in their subject | 3 | 54.9 | 40.1 |
| They maintain and improve their subject knowledge on a regular basis | 1 | 44.4 | 35.7 |
| They have received training in how to teach | 7 | 24.8 | 22.2 |

| | Rank (out of 21 subjects) | %<br>History students | All students |
|---|---|---|---|
| **Teaching (continued)** | | | |
| They have relevant industry or professional expertise | 11 | 40.0 | 43.2 |
| They employ original/creative teaching methods | 13 | 15.0 | 15.0 |
| They maintain and improve their teaching skills on a regular basis | 4 | 21.6 | 18.3 |
| **Feedback** | | | |

**Q10c.1. Thinking about all the teaching you have experienced this academic year, what proportion of teaching staff did the following? (answering all/majority)**

| | Rank | History students | All students |
|---|---|---|---|
| Were open to having further discussions about your work (giving extra feedback) | 1 | 77.2 | 57.5 |
| Gave you useful feedback | 1 | 73.4 | 54.1 |
| Gave you feedback in time to help you with the next assignment | 1 | 65.0 | 52.5 |
| Put a lot of time into commenting on your work | 1 | 59.0 | 36.2 |
| Gave you more general feedback on your progress | 3 | 45.3 | 39.9 |
| Gave you feedback on draft work (or discussed assignments while you were working on them) | 3 | 40.2 | 33.8 |

**Q10b. How do you normally receive feedback on assignments?**

| | Rank | History students | All students |
|---|---|---|---|
| In person | 3 | 35.6 | 20.8 |
| Written comments only | 15 | 15.6 | 16.9 |
| Grade only (no written comments) | 21 | 3.5 | 14.1 |

| | Rank (out of 21 subjects) | % History students | All students |
|---|---|---|---|
| **Feedback (continued)** | | | |
| Written comments and a grade | 6 | 69.9 | 64.7 |
| By email | 12 | 17.8 | 19.3 |
| Other | 19 | 3.7 | 5.0 |
| Don't know | 21 | 0.2 | 0.7 |

**Overall satisfaction**

**Q12. Thinking back to when you applied to your current university, has the reality of your academic experience matched your expectations?**

| | | | |
|---|---|---|---|
| It's been better | 1 | 32.2 | 26.0 |

**Q12e. Since starting your course, do you feel you have learned:**

| | | | |
|---|---|---|---|
| A lot | 5 | 70.1 | 65.3 |

**Q12b.i. Thinking about your academic experience, knowing what you know now, if you had a second chance to start again, would you do any of the following?**

| | | | |
|---|---|---|---|
| No change | 5 | 69.4 | 66.4 |

**Q16. Thinking of all the things you've been asked about in this questionnaire so far, which statement best describes your view of the value for money of your present course?**

| | | | |
|---|---|---|---|
| Good/very good | 16 | 35.1 | 41.0 |
| Poor/very poor | 5 | 34.1 | 28.4 |

# ENDNOTES

1   John Rowe, n.d., 'What employers want: thoughts from a history BA in business', AHA (https://bit.ly/3a5RND3).

2   Frank Valadez, n.d., 'The well-rounded history graduate: professional, citizen, human', AHA (https://bit.ly/2HPCRwv).

3   Chris C. and Dan Sharp, cited in Marcus Collins, 'Historiography from below: how undergraduates remember learning history at school', *Teaching History* **142**(2011), 35–6.

4   Sam Wineburg, *Why Learn History (When It's Already on Your Phone)* (Chicago, IL: University of Chicago Press, 2018), part 3.

5   This thought was attributed to the famous Greek historian Thucydides in Dionysius of Halicarnassus (attrib.), *Ars Rhetorica,* tr. William H. Race (Cambridge, MA: Harvard University Press, 2019).

6   George Santayana, *The Life of Reason,* vol. I (New York: Charles Scribner's, 1917), 284.

7   This poll was taken in 2018 in the Osher Lifelong Learning Institute, associated with George Mason University.

8   Michael Pavkovic and Stephen Morillo, *What Is Military History?* (Cambridge: Polity Press, 2018).

9   On the uses and misuses of analogy, see Ernest May and Richard Neustadt, *Thinking in Time: The Uses of History for Decision-Makers* (New York: Free Press, 1988).

10  Martin Sherwin, 2017, 'What the Cuban Missile Crisis can teach us about the North Korean Missile Crisis to avoid catastrophe', *The Nation,* August 23 (https://bit.ly/38WkEt1).

11  In *Thinking in Time*, Ernest May and Richard Neustadt trace the dubious fate of the Munich analogy. Rethinking the analogy entered strongly into 'revisionist' interpretations of the Cold War; see Walter LaFeber, *America, Russia and the Cold War* (New York: Wiley, 1967).

12  The classic work on the role of history and historical distortion in nationalism is Benedict Anderson, *Imagined Communities: Reflections on the Origins and Spread of Nationalism* (London: Verso, 1991).

13  Fay Bound Alberti, *A Biography of Loneliness: The History of an Emotion* (Oxford: Oxford University Press, 2019).

14  On Western attitudes to nature, see Lynn White, *Medieval Technology and Social Change* (New York: Oxford University Press, 1982).

15  Aditi Malhotra, 2018, 'What Indian parents want most for their children', *Wall Street Journal*, April 3. See also Peter Stearns, 'Happy children: a modern emotional commitment', *Frontiers In Psychology* **10**(2019) (https://doi.org/10.3389/fpsyg.2019.02025).

16  Darrin McMahon, *Happiness: A History* (New York: Atlantic Monthly Press, 2005).

17  On Cicero's belief in the importance of history, see Elizabeth Rawson, 'Cicero the historian and Cicero the antiquarian', *Journal of Roman Studies* **62**(1972), 33–45.

18  Denise Bentrovato, ed., *History Can Bite: History Education in Divided and Postwar Societies* (Göttingen: V&R unipress, 2016).

19  This course, offered by Mills Kelly, occasioned major controversy. See Yoni Appelbaum, 2012, 'How the professor who fooled Wikipedia got caught by Reddit', *The Atlantic*, May 15 (https://bit.ly/2vZYVlD). See also T. Mills Kelly, 2014, 'Lying about the past', *Change: The Magazine of Higher Learning* **46**(4), 14–15.

20  See, for example, Libby Sander, 2017, 'In the workplace of the future, these are the skills employers want', World Economic Forum and *The Conversation*, March 7 (https://bit.ly/3bZRTh8). The study cites data suggesting that demand for critical thinking skills on the part of junior employees had gone up 158% in Australia during the three previous years.

21    Angira Patel, 2018, 'To be a good doctor, study the humanities', *Pacific Standard*, May 23 (https://bit.ly/2TdhYk3).

22    Paul B. Sturtevant, 2017, 'History is not a useless major: fighting myths with data', *AHA Perspectives*, April 1 (https://bit.ly/2Vk7FNU).

23    This figure refers to 'terminal' history BA students, who did not progress to graduate school, and is derived from Humanities Indicators, 2018, 'Earnings of humanities majors with a terminal bachelor's degree', American Academy of Arts & Sciences (https://bit.ly/3c2OQ7V).

24    Humanities Indicators, 2015, 'Humanities majors and the Law School Admission Test (LSAT)', American Academy of Arts & Sciences (https://bit.ly/3bZTQds); Humanities Indicators, 2015, 'Humanities majors and the Graduate Management Admission Test (GMAT)', American Academy of Arts & Sciences (https://bit.ly/37Vq5Y7); Humanities Indicators, 2015, 'Humanities majors and the Medical College Admission Test (MCAT)', American Academy of Arts & Sciences (https://bit.ly/3c7zu2a).

25    Anthony P. Carnevale, Ban Cheah and Martin Van Der Werf, *ROI of Liberal Arts Colleges: Value Adds Up over Time* (Washington, DC: Georgetown University Center on Education and the Workforce, 2020).

26    These figures were derived from Department for Education, 2019, 'Employment and earnings outcomes of higher education graduates: experimental data from the Longitudinal Education Outcomes (LEO) dataset, 2016–17 tax year' (https://bit.ly/2XA12Z3).

27    Jack Britton, Lorraine Dearden, Laura van der Erve and Ben Waltmann, *The Impact of Undergraduate Degrees on Lifetime Earnings* (London: Institute for Fiscal Studies/Department for Education, 2020).

28    Gallup and Purdue University, *Great Jobs, Great Lives: The 2014 Gallup–Purdue Index Report* (Washington, DC: Gallup, 2014), 11.

29    Humanities Indicators, 2018, 'Job satisfaction of humanities majors', American Academy of Arts & Sciences, June (https://bit.ly/2Pk466q).

30    Benjamin Schmidt, 2018, 'The humanities are in crisis', *The Atlantic*, August 23 (https://bit.ly/2SRDeNw).

31  Gallup and Lumina Foundation, *Americans Value Postsecondary Education: The 2015 Gallup–Lumina Foundation Study of the American Public's Opinion on Higher Education* (Washington, DC: Gallup, 2018), 10.

32  Strada Education Network and Gallup, *From College to Life: Relevance and the Value of Higher Education* (Washington, DC: Gallup, 2018), 5.

33  Loren Collins, 2015, 'Entering the job market with a BA in history', *AHA Today*, May 12 (https://bit.ly/2w2bbBS).

34  Ibid.

35  Staci Heidtke, 2015, 'Career planning as an undergraduate in history', *AHA Today*, June 1 (https://bit.ly/3c0oTWt).

36  Katharine Brooks, *You Majored in What? Mapping Your Path from Chaos to Career* (New York: Viking ebook, 2009), ch. 5.

37  Ibid., ch.11.

38  See, for example, John S. Bowman, ed., *Columbia Chronologies of Asian History and Culture* (New York: Columbia University Press, 2000).

39  For major discoveries on the origins of modern consumerism, see Neil McKendrick, Colin Brewer and J. H. Plumb, *The Birth of a Consumer Society: The Commercialization of Eighteenth-Century England* (Bloomington, IN: Indiana University Press, 1982). On the 'industrious revolution' as an example of changing ideas on periodization, see Jan de Vries, *The Industrious Revolution: Consumer Behaviour and the Household Economy, 1650 to the Present* (Cambridge: Cambridge University Press, 2008), and Akira Hayami, *Japan's Industrious Revolution: Economic and Social Transformations in the Early Modern Period* (New York: Springer, 2015).

40  'Data: most states require history, but not civics', *Education Week*, October 23, 2018 (https://bit.ly/39ZQbKL).

41  David Christian and William H. McNeill, *Maps of Time: An Introduction to Big History*, 2nd edn (Berkeley, CA: University of California Press, 2011).

42  Exemplary comparative studies include David Brion Davis, *The Problem of Slavery in the Age of Emancipation* (New York: Vintage, 2015); Seymour

Drescher, *Abolition: A History of Slavery and Antislavery* (Cambridge: Cambridge University Press, 2009); Theda Skocpol, *States and Social Revolutions: A Comparative Analysis of France, Russia, and China* (Cambridge: Cambridge University Press, 2015); Karen Offen, 1988, 'Defining feminism: a comparative historical approach', *Signs* **14**(1), 119–57.

43    Jason Reid, *Get Out of My Room! A History of Teen Bedrooms in America* (Chicago, IL: University of Chicago Press, 2017).

44    James Grossman, 2015, 'Everything has a history', *Perspectives on History*, December 1 (https://bit.ly/3c1AYe5).

45    Geoffrey R. Elton, *The Practice of History*, 2nd edn (Oxford: Wiley-Blackwell, 1991); Charles Maier, *Leviathan 2.0: Inventing Modern Statehood* (Cambridge, MA: Belknap, 2014); James Patterson, 'The persistence of political history, in Richard Kirkendall, ed., *The Organization of American Historians and the Writing and Teaching of American History* (New York: Oxford University Press, 2011).

46    Jeremy Black, *A History of Diplomacy* (London: Reaktion, 2011); Lloyd Gardner, Walter LaFeber and Thomas McCormick, *Creation of the American Empire II: U.S. Diplomatic History Since 1893* (Chicago, IL: Rand McNally, 1979).

47    See Frederick Kagan, 2006, 'Why military history matters', American Enterprise Institute, June 27 (https://bit.ly/38XsWB1). See also Pavkovic and Morillo, *What Is Military History?* (endnote 8).

48    Scott Manning, 2009, 'What is the value of studying military history', *Historian on the Warpath*, October 15 (https://bit.ly/2HUw3O4).

49    Thomas S. Kuhn, *The Structure of Scientific Revolutions*, 3rd edn (Chicago, IL: University of Chicago Press, 1996).

50    Robert Darnton and Daniel Roche, eds, *Revolution in Print: The Press in France 1775–1800* (Berkeley, CA: University of Chicago Press, 1989).

51    Good introductions include Kelly Grovier, *A New Way of Seeing the History of Art in 57 Works* (London: Thames and Hudson, 2019); Will Gompertz, *What Are You Looking At? The Surprising, Shocking and Sometimes Strange Story of 150 Years of Modern Art* (New York: Dutton, 2012); Helen Gardner and Fred Kleiner, *Gardner's Art Through the Ages: A Global History*, 14th edn (Boston, MA: Wadsworth, 2013).

52  See Jesse Lemisch, 'The American revolution seen from the bottom up', in Barton J. Bernstein, ed., *Towards a New Past: Dissenting Essays in American History* (New York: Pantheon Books, 1968), 3–45.

53  E. P. Thompson, *The Making of the English Working Class* (New York: Vintage, 1966), 12; special issue of the *Journal of Social History* **29**(1995).

54  Merry Wiesner-Hanks, *Gender in History: Global Perspectives*, 2nd edn (Malden, MA: Wiley, 2010).

55  The possibility of marrying the work of quantitative historians with the opportunities presented by Big Data is just now gaining attention, and it bears watching in future. Big Data in the social sciences are almost always historical, on voting behaviours, population changes, crime rates, etc. This also applies to data useful in business, e.g. consumer patterns over time. However, historians are only now recognizing Big Data's potential role and the career opportunities that might result. For some important comment, see Jo Guldi and David Armitage, *The History Manifesto* (Cambridge: Cambridge University Press, 2012).

56  Victoria Bonnell and Lynn Hunt, eds, *Beyond the Cultural Turn: New Directions in the Study of Society and Culture* (Berkeley, CA: University of California Press, 1999); Peter N. Stearns, *Culture Change in Modern World History* (London: Bloomsbury, 2018). For a classic study, see Keith Thomas, *Religion and the Decline of Magic* (London: Penguin, 2003).

57  For a half-decent effort in this vein, see Marcus Collins, *The Beatles and Sixties Britain* (Cambridge: Cambridge University Press, 2020).

58  Ludmilla Jordanova, *History in Practice* (London: Hodder Arnold, 2005); Ian Tyrrell, *Historians in Public: The Practice of American History* (Chicago, IL: University of Chicago Press, 2005); Guy Beiner, *Forgetful Remembrance: Social Forgetting and a Vernacular Historiography of a Rebellion in Ulster* (Oxford: Oxford University Press, 2018); Cathy Stanton, *The Lowell Experiment: Public History in a Postindustrial City* (Amherst, MA: University of Massachusetts Press, 2006).

59  See, for example, the activities of the oral history society, formed in 1973 as an offshoot of the British Institute of Recorded Sound.

60  T. Mills Kelly, *Teaching History in a Digital Age* (Ann Arbor, MI: University of Michigan Press, digitalculturebooks, 2013).

61  See HyperStudio's Chronos Timeline, MIT (https://bit.ly/2vkgRr3).

62  John McNeill and Peter Engelke, *The Great Acceleration: An Environmental History of the Anthropocene Since 1945* (Cambridge, MA: Harvard University Press, 2016).

63  Donald Worster, ed., *The Ends of the Earth: Perspectives on Modern Environmental History* (Cambridge: Cambridge University Press, 1988), Introduction.

64  See https://research.uta.fi/hex/, the website for the Centre of Excellence in History of Experiences (HEX) at Tampere University.

65  Mark Smith, *Sensing the Past: Seeing, Hearing, Smelling, Tasting and Touching in History* (Berkeley, CA: University of California Press, 2007).

66  A. Roger Ekrich, *At Day's Close: Night in Times Past* (London: W. W. Norton, 2006).

67  Rob Boddice, *A History of Feelings* (London: Reaktion, 2019); Luke Fernandez and Susan Matt, *Bored, Lonely, Angry, Stupid: Changing Feelings about Technology from the Telegraph to Twitter* (Cambridge, MA: Harvard University Press, 2019).

68  Marcus Collins, *Modern Love: An Intimate History of Men and Women in Twentieth-Century Britain* (London: Atlantic, 2003).

69  Peter N. Stearns, *Shame: A Brief History* (Urbana, IL: University of Illinois Press, 2017).

70  Student Academic Experience Survey, 2014–19.

71  Jaimie Francis and Zac Auter, n.d., '3 ways to realign higher education with today's workforce', *Gallup News* (https://bit.ly/2PinYXW).

72  Gallup and Lumina Foundation, *Americans Value Postsecondary Education: The 2015 Gallup–Lumina Foundation Study of the American Public's Opinion on Higher Education* (Washington, DC: Gallup, 2018), 6.

73  See 'Major exploration' on the La Verne University website (https://bit.ly/2VhdZWp).

74  Steve Crabtree, 2019, 'Students at smaller colleges more likely to say faculty care', *Gallup News*, January 30 (https://bit.ly/2PlZexL).

75  See 'Information for new students' on the Whitman College website (https://bit.ly/2VhdtrB).

76  Zac Auter, 2017, 'What Gallup learned about higher education in 2017', *Gallup News*, December 27 (https://bit.ly/2T9wKZj).

77  See American Historical Association, 2016, 'AHA History Tuning Project: 2016 history discipline core' (https://bit.ly/3c5EwMw).

78  Marcus Collins and Adele Nye, 'The discipline of history in British and Australian universities', in Jennifer Clark and Adele Nye, eds, *Teaching and Learning History in the Modern University: Disciplining History* (New York: Springer, 2018), 35.

79  Gallup and Purdue University, *Great Jobs, Great Lives*, 5 (endnote 26).

80  Brandon Busteed, 2017, '5 ways to make college a success', *Gallup News*, June 6 (https://bit.ly/2T9FnmK).

81  Strada Education Network and Gallup, *Mentoring College Students to Success: The 2018 Strada–Gallup Alumni Survey* (Washington, DC: Gallup, 2018), 7.

82  Steve Crabtree, 2019, 'Student support from faculty, mentors varies by major', *Gallup News*, January 24 (https://bit.ly/39X9rsv).

83  NACE Staff, 2019, 'Converting interns, co-ops into full-time hires on the rise', National Association of Colleges and Employers, April 12 (https://bit.ly/2SUcagF).

84  Sam Wineburg, *Historical Thinking and Other Unnatural Acts* (Philadelphia, PA: Temple University Press, 2011).

85  Karina Korostelina, *History Can Bite: History Education in Divided and Post-War Societies* (Göttingen: Vandenhoeck and Ruprecht, 2016).

86  Joy Masoff, cited in Kevin Sieff, 2010, 'Virginia 4th-grade textbook criticized over claims on black Confederate soldiers', *Washington Post*, October 20 (https://wapo.st/2Vkd9bI).

87  Hence the statement by the Chancellor of Germany in 2019 after visiting a Holocaust site: 'This site obliges us to keep the memory alive. We must remember the crimes that were committed here and name them clearly.'

(Cited in Kate Connolly, 2019, 'Angela Merkel speaks of "deep shame" on first visit to Auschwitz', *The Guardian*, December 6 (https://bit.ly/2Pm2c5w).)

88    Patrick Collison and Tyler Cowen, 2019, 'We need a new science of progress: humanity needs to get better at knowing how to get better', *The Atlantic*, July 30 (https://bit.ly/2vbNKWQ).

89    David Ignatius, 2015, 'Five peace agreements to use as guides for a post-Islamic State Middle East', *Washington Post*, November 19. See also Patrick Milton, Michael Axworthy and Brendan Simms, *Towards a Westphalia for the Middle East* (New York: Hurst, 2020).

90    Lizabeth Cohen, 2019, 'The midcentury battle to save America's cities from crisis', *Literary Hub*, October 8 (https://bit.ly/2HNiAI6).

91    *History and Policy*, n.d. (www.historyandpolicy.org/); *Checkered History: Home of The Political Uses of the Past Project*, n.d. (http://historychecked.com/).

92    For one of many available studies on this topic, see Samuel Cohn, *Epidemics: Hate and Compassion from the Plague of Athens to AIDS* (Oxford: Oxford University Press, 2018).

93    Jill Lepore, *This America: The Case for the Nation* (New York: Liveright, 2019).

94    On nostalgia and family history, see Stephanie Coontz, *Marriage, A History: How Love Conquered Marriage* (New York: Penguin, 2019).

95    Steven Pinker, *Enlightenment Now: The Case for Reason, Science, Humanism and Progress* (New York: Penguin, 2018). Many reviews by historians have been critical of Pinker's evidence and arguments; see Jessica Riskin, 2019, 'Pinker's Pollyannish philosophy and its perfidious politics', *Los Angeles Review of Books*, December 15 (https://bit.ly/2vbp6ph).

96    Fiona Hill, 2019, 'Opening statement', *Politico*, November 21 (https://politi.co/38WOEoG).

# ABOUT THE AUTHORS

MARCUS COLLINS is Senior Lecturer in Cultural History at Loughborough University and an elected member of the Council of the Royal Historical Society. A specialist on popular culture and social change in Britain since 1945, he is the author of *The Beatles and Sixties Britain* (Cambridge University Press, 2020) and *Modern Love: An Intimate History of Men and Women in Twentieth-Century Britain* (Atlantic Books, 2003), and the editor of *The Permissive Society and Its Enemies: Sixties British Culture* (Rivers Oram Press, 2007).

PETER N. STEARNS is University Professor of History at George Mason University. He teaches undergraduate courses on world history and on US and comparative social and cultural history, including the history of emotion. He also regularly collaborates on undergraduate research. He has authored or edited more than 140 books and had great fun working on his most recent: *Time in World History* (Routledge, 2019). His new edited collection, *Death in Modern World History*, will be published in autumn 2020.